Shell of an Idea

The untold history of PowerShell

Don Jones

Shell of an Idea

The untold history of PowerShell

Don Jones

ISBN 978-1-953645-03-6

Also By Don Jones

The DSC Book

The PowerShell Scripting and Toolmaking Book

Become Hardcore Extreme Black Belt PowerShell Ninja Rockstar

Don Jones' PowerShell 4N00bs

Instructional Design for Mortals

How to Find a Wolf in Siberia

Tales of the Icelandic Troll

PowerShell by Mistake

The Culture of Learning

Alabaster

Power Wave

The Never

Onyx

Sparks!

Superior Wave

Verdant

To the PowerShell team, past and present. For all you've done, and for all you'll do, thank you.

Contents

Foreword

Nietzsche once said, "What we do is never understood, but only praised or blamed." There are people that praise PowerShell and there are people that blame PowerShell, but few people understand PowerShell. One of those few is Don Jones. It is hard to overstate Don's importance in the PowerShell story; he is the proverbial "First Follower." (Do yourself a favor and spend three minutes searching for a video called "First Follower: Leadership Lessons from Dancing Guy" and watch it now. No—I mean "now." I'll wait.)

I met Don in a bar in Las Vegas. He told me he wrote books—"really fast and really good." He said he understood IT pros, that they were going to love Monad, but that it would take 10 years before it became mainstream. I told him he was wrong and explained all the things we were doing to avoid the "crossing the chasm" problem. As I recall, his response was "Ok. Sure." If you've never talked with Don, it is hard to convey his ability to politely tell you that you are full of it, but it isn't worth his time or effort to explain it to you. If you hear "OK" *or* "Sure" you are really in the weeds, but "Ok. Sure." is a clue. You can guess where this story is going. In the end, Don was right—about that and so many other things along the way. It is a good thing I ignored him because if I had a clue about the difficulty that was in store for us on the path to take the great ideas in Monad and ship it as PowerShell, I would have ordered us another round and moved on to something else.

In *Shell of an Idea,* Don tells some of the many stories behind the creation of PowerShell and its design. It is a story of a group of amazing engineers struggling to forge a whole suite of new technologies into a coherent experience—all the while fighting a multi-year game of internal politics whack-a-mole. In case it is not clear—we were the moles. Microsoft's embrace and mastery of

GUIs brought it such overwhelming success that it was found to be a monopoly. So when I came to the company talking about the importance of command line interfaces and programmatic shells… well you can imagine how well that went over. The only reason we were funded to do a shell was to compete with Linux and even then, it was deemed so unimportant that I had to take a demotion to work on it full time.

The world has an unfortunate habit of giving all the credit to a single hero. The reality is that big things happen because of teams. So it is with PowerShell. I came up with several of the core foundational concepts and architectural principles, but PowerShell is unequivocally the product of a team of awesome engineers. Bill Gates used to say that Microsoft was great at finding and hiring the world's best software talent but failed at getting their IQs to add up. I am most proud I was able to create an environment that allowed a group of some of the world's best engineers to ship their ideas in a way that their IQs added up. This book is the story of those engineers, their ideas, and the messy path to adding it all up and shipping in an environment actively trying to kill the project at every step along the way.

Jeffrey Snover
May 2020

Introduction

My history with Windows administrative automation goes back a long way, at least to my 2003 book, *Managing Windows with VBScript and WMI* (Addison-Wesley). A bestseller of the time, it put me on the map as someone who spoke about, taught, and wrote about Windows automation. It helped drive my first Microsoft MVP Award recognition in 2004 and made it natural for me to jump into Windows PowerShell–then called Monad–when it hit the scene in 2005.

I was honored to co-present with Jeffrey Snover at TechEd Europe 2006 in Barcelona, where Microsoft formally launched PowerShell and introduced it to the world. I wrote the first published book on PowerShell, *Windows PowerShell: TFM* (SAPIEN Press) and have in total written or co-authored close to a dozen books on PowerShell. *Learn Windows PowerShell in a Month of Lunches* (Manning Books) remains a go-to bestseller for newcomers, and *PowerShell In Depth* (Manning) is still a top reference for PowerShell admins. I co-founded PowerShell.org, launched the PowerShell + DevOps Global Summit with my partner, and was named "PowerShell's First Follower" by Jeffrey Snover at the first Microsoft Ignite events in Chicago. I coined the terms "Toolmaker" and "Toolmaking" within the PowerShell world, and have been an advocate for strong practices and patterns. I even substituted for Jeffrey Snover as a speaker at the TechEd North America 2007 conference. Suffice to say that PowerShell has been an *enormous* part of my life and career.

Over the years, I've made a ton of good friends in the PowerShell community, which is easily one of the friendliest and most down-to-earth group of technologists I've ever met. My office has a small collection of the thoughtful, tongue-in-cheek mementos they've given me: a CIA challenge coin, a Lego minifig of myself, a beer stein with PowerShell and Disney's Figment character etched into it, and more. My career has taken me away from the day-to-day engagements with both the technology and that audience, but they've both been such a huge part of my life and career that I can never step fully away.

In fact, that was the genesis for this book: I just can't let PowerShell go. It's not only been important to me, but it's also been hugely important and impactful to so many people in the industry. And yet PowerShell almost never happened. In fact, it almost never happened more than once. Were it not for a team of passionate visionaries willing to make the occasional possibly-career-limiting moves, PowerShell–and all the positive impact it's created–wouldn't have existed. PowerShell might have just been a port of Unix' KornShell, or it might have just been a WMI querying tool. Or it might not have been a thing at all.

There's a lot of untold story under the shell, and it's a story I wanted to tell. Much of PowerShell's core team have moved on to other teams or even to other companies. Nobody's getting any younger. I felt it was time to capture their stories and the shell's story while I could still track everyone down. Some bits of the story have been told at conferences or in other venues, but it's never been pulled together into one place–and it's never been told in its entirety.

If you've worked with PowerShell, then *Shell of an Idea* should provide some fascinating backstory to it. If you haven't worked with PowerShell but you're at least conversant with computers and systems administration, then you're in for a real treat. As much as possible I've tried to wrap context around the stories so that you can see where they fit into the world, and what PowerShell struggled against and sought to solve.

I've also included a number of quotes, solicited through my blog at DonJones.com[1]. These may seem out of context as I present them,

---

[1]http://donjones.com

but they're intended to provide some background for the people that PowerShell has impacted the most. I've edited these as lightly as possible for length and clarity because I feel that the effect of the shell's story is just as important as the story itself. Here's one example:

> PowerShell changed my life... I realize that such a statement may seem exaggerated, but every Powershell enthusiast can relate in some way to the overwhelming benefits and career opportunities that learning Power-Shell has given them.
>
> I had worked in an operations management position for five years and dreaded going into work every day. The stress was awful, but the monotony was worse. I was 30 years old, had a wife and two boys under two years old, and living on my single income. I was afraid it was too late to change careers and find work I actually enjoyed. However, my older brother who worked as a system administrator for a large tech company told me about how he used PowerShell in his job and loved it. He was a PowerShell enthusiast and thought I could learn it and open up an opportunity to change into the IT field. He actually gave me the book he used that helped him learn, *Learn PowerShell In a Month of Lunches*.
>
> That was about six months ago, and I was fortunate that an opportunity opened up at my current company in our IT department soon after I started learning. The little I knew at the time allowed me to get my foot in the door and gave me the opportunity to make an immediate impact and learn in a practical way.
>
> PowerShell is easy to learn, incredibly practical, and useful in most every environment. Since I started, I've scripted automated tasks that run daily, created GUI tools for our Operations department and many more

things like interacting with web APIs, and more.

I now love what I do, and I'm excited about the career and financial opportunities this new path will help provide for me and my family. I will forever be a PowerShell evangelist and look forward to continuing to gain a more in-depth knowledge, and hopefully have the opportunity to teach and train others on how Powershell can potentially change their lives as well.

–Aaron

How can you not want to read more of the story of a technology that can generate that kind of feeling? "Easy to learn," "incredibly practical," and "I now love what I do;" those aren't statements we often see all attached to a single technology, right? The journey to create a product that engenders those remarks must be amazing.

It's easy, as we sit in front of our monitors and tap away on our phones, to forget that the story of technology is a story of people. It's about visionaries who see problems and try to solve them, who take on some small piece of the world and try to make it at least a little better. It can be difficult for us everyday folks to look at the end result and be impressed by it. What I hope you take away from this book, though, is that those amazing end results come in tiny, often-difficult steps. If you're willing to take those little steps and push through the hurdles, you can make just as big of a difference. The people who brought PowerShell to life are just ordinary people who shared a vision and worked hard to make it a reality.

This is their story, and I'm proud to share it. I hope you enjoy it.

Don Jones

Cast of Characters

While dozens, if not hundreds, of people helped bring PowerShell to life, these are the ones you'll see mentioned most prominently in this book. They were in key leadership and management positions during PowerShell's earliest days, and many of them stayed with PowerShell well into its open-source, cross-platform days. This list is by no means exhaustive, but it does represent the primary interview sources for this book. This list is alphabetical by surname.

- Charlie Chase - Group Program Manager (helped bring PowerShell into Exchange Server and eventually Windows)
- Kenneth Hansen - Program Manager (throughout the Monad period and into PowerShell 6), no longer at Microsoft
- Lee Holmes - Software Engineer (responsible for much of PowerShell's security design)
- Hemant Mahawar - Program Manager (throughout the Monad period and into PowerShell 6), no longer at Microsoft
- Bruce Payette - Lead Developer (responsible for much of PowerShell's language design, also designed the original Desired State Configuration), no longer at Microsoft
- Jeffrey Snover - Architect (the inventor of PowerShell; turned Kermit into Monad, wrote the Monad Manifesto, and championed Monad and PowerShell from the outset)
- Jim Truher - Program Manager (very much the "PowerShell archivist" and one of the original Monad team members)
- Daryl Wray - Program Manager (originator of the Kermit project, convinced by Snover to flip to Monad), now retired

These are by no means all the people who contributed to Monad and PowerShell. Countless software engineers, documentation specialists, program managers, testers, and more worked long and hard to bring the product to life and to evolve it over time. Anyone involved with the PowerShell community back in the day will recognize names like June Blender, Dan Harman, Hilal Al-Hilali, Erin Chapple, Refaat Issa, and more. A new guard is shepherding PowerShell today, including people like Michael Greene, Joey Aiello, Jason Helmick, and many others. The list above simply represents the cast of characters who contributed anecdotes and timelines to this book, and constitutes some of the most influential and community-involved names of the time.

There are some ancillary names that will come up. Ironically most of these names, due to their positions within Microsoft at the time, are probably better-known. I'll attempt to get their titles or positions correct for the time in which PowerShell was being created:

- Jim Allchin - Led the Platforms division at Microsoft. Left Microsoft in 2007.
- Bob Muglia - President in charge of Windows Server and other divisions, reported to CEO Steve Ballmer. Left Microsoft in 2011.
- Steven Sinofsky - Vice President in charge of Windows during the PowerShell v3 timeframe. Left Microsoft in 2015.
- S. Somasegar - Leader of Developer Division, founder of the India Development Center. Left Microsoft in 2015.
- Dave Thompson - Held a variety of positions during the early PowerShell years, including leadership in the Windows (2000-2004) and Exchange Server (2004-2011) teams. Left Microsoft in 2011.
- Brian Valentine - Led the Exchange team from v4 through v5.5; led Windows Client and Server teams. Left Microsoft in 2006.

HISTORY

A Shell of a Problem

"All I have to do is push a button on each one..."

To understand the history of PowerShell and its subsequent impact, you need to understand a bit of Microsoft history. At least, a simplified version of a tiny piece of it.

Until 1993, Microsoft Windows was a desktop operating system, meaning it ran on individual computers used by individual people. Most of those computers were fairly large, beige boxes that sat on or under a desk. Laptop computers at the time were pretty primitive and bulky compared to what you might see today. The Windows of the day was v3.1, and it couldn't even participate fully in the more primitive computer networks of the day. Home users tended to rely on dial-up services like America Online rather than the always-on Internet we take for granted these days. That Windows was shortly succeeded by Windows for Workgroups, the first fully network-capable Windows operating environment and the first Windows arguably created with business scenarios specifically in mind. But even then, Windows for Workgroups could really only *join* a network; there was no version of Windows capable of *hosting* a network. Networks of the time were hosted by a server, with the most common servers running either a product called NetWare 3.1, produced by a company called Novell, or a variant of the UNIX operating system.

Unix (as it is more commonly styled nowadays) had been around for a while by then, primarily at military research facilities and large universities but also running on the enormously expensive mainframe[2] and midrange computers used by the largest enterprise companies. It featured robust networking, and in fact provided the underpinnings of what would become today's Internet. Unix at the time was both incredibly complex to use (compared to Windows) and incredibly expensive; a single Unix computer could easily represent an investment in the tens of thousands of dollars, and required specialized training to operate.

NetWare was common in small- and medium-sized businesses. It was fairly complex to install and manage, and it included its own protocols for network communications. NetWare could run on smaller, cheaper computers, and it was somewhat simpler for network administrators to learn to use.

Perhaps most importantly, many decent-sized companies didn't have a network at all; they had a midrange computer like an IBM

---

[2]To be fair, these were technically "minicomputers," but the word "mini" in our modern context completely understates the size and cost of the things. I'll incorrectly refer to them as "mainframes" just to help set the right tone.

AS/400[3] that handled all of the business's computing. Users connected to these midrange computers through "terminal emulation" cards that plugged into their bulky desktop computers, and by using applications that ran on Windows. Essentially, these terminal emulators turned each desktop into a "dumb monitor" (literally not much more than a television hardwired to the midrange machine) capable of sending keystrokes and displaying whatever the midrange sent back. Truly huge companies often had a mainframe that was basically just a giant equivalent to a midrange, such as the Digital Equipment VAX line of computers. Again, people often connected to these via "dumb terminals" that were wired directly to the computer.

The point is that in the early 1990s computer networking wasn't a big thing for most businesses, and you needed specialized personnel to build and run a network if you did have one. It wasn't like today, where your smartphone can join a wireless network with a couple of taps, and you can set up your own home WiFi network just by plugging in a box and running a setup application on your phone.

So, the landscape of the time: big companies had a single enormous computer, and perhaps a bunch of pricey Unix machines [4] to supplement it. Smaller companies maybe had a few Windows or MS-DOS desktop computers connected to a NetWare server. Without networking, it was a pretty big pain to own more than a handful of computers, and so nobody really bothered. Even a giant tech university like MIT could probably have counted up all the computers they owned without much effort–a marked contrast to today's world, where most of us have a pocket computer (called a smartphone), maybe a laptop or tablet, maybe a wrist computer (smart watch), a gaming machine, and more. In the early 1990s, a single human being didn't run around owning a half dozen computers. Today, we probably can't accurately count how many

---

[3]These are referred to as IBM's System i computers now, after having briefly been rebranded to iSeries.

[4]Unix workstations were sized more like a modern PC, but still cost thousands and thousands of dollars.

of them are on the planet.

In 1993 Microsoft launched Windows NT, its first truly business-grade edition of Windows. Most critically, it launched Windows NT Server, which was their first operating system capable of hosting a robust network. Windows NT wasn't yet anywhere near the class of a midrange or mainframe operating system, but it could certainly compete with Novell NetWare as the centerpiece of a small- or medium-sized business network. Even large companies started buying Windows NT, but not to replace their AS/400 or VAX machine, mind you! In most cases, Windows NT snuck into the environment, purchased by a single department that was tired of not getting the computing resources they wanted from their company's midrange or mainframe. Compared to NetWare, Windows NT was easy to set up and straightforward to operate. It adopted the same graphical user interface that had made Windows so popular on the desktop. It was an easy sell: "add a file or print network as easily as opening up your word processor!"

This was a truly critical point in computing history: suddenly, *everyone* could have a server capable of hosting shared files, providing shared printing services, and other basic tasks. Servers were cheaper, and Windows NT made it easy for almost anyone to set up a network. Network computing had been democratized and commoditized, and almost every business wanted in on it. The number of servers installed in the world's companies began to proliferate *markedly*. Microsoft followed Windows NT (initially versioned 3.1) with Windows NT 3.51 and then Windows NT 4. Dropping the "NT," they then followed with Windows 2000 Server and then Windows Server 2003.

By 2003, Windows–and the many applications that ran on it–had grown up a *lot*. It was fully capable of taking on numerous enterprise-class workloads such as messaging, collaboration, databases, and more. Microsoft–themselves an AS/400 company for much of their history–committed to running their own company on Windows Server, and had made the jump by the 2003-2005 timeframe.

Here's the advantage of moving your computing from giant, million-dollar AS/400 and VAX systems to smaller, commodity servers running Windows Server: it's cheaper. Sure, a single Windows Server might not be able to do messaging *and* filing *and* printing *and* databases *and* whatever else, but you could buy three dozen Windows Server machines for *far* less than the price of a single AS/400. In the late 1990s, as the public Internet and World Wide Web came online and proliferated, people quickly realized that having *more, cheaper* servers was often better than having one expensive one. Want to stand up a website that can survive the traffic when your company gets mentioned on Oprah? Have that website served up by an entire building full of cheap web servers, each taking a small part of the overall workload. Today's cloud, in the form of Amazon Web Services, Microsoft Azure, Google Cloud, and others, exists entirely around the concept of "lots of cheap computers."

But here's the downside of all those servers: someone has to manage them. They need to be configured to work properly, and they need to *stay* configured. They need periodic security updates and bug patches. Patching one server back in 1994 was no big deal, but patching a building containing thousands of servers in 2003 became an entirely different thing.

And that's where Windows Server ran into trouble.

Sure, Windows Server was "as easy to run as the desktop you already know and love," but the ability to click through a wizard to install a patch didn't scale well. Having to run through the same wizard on ten computers–clicking Next, Next, Next, Next, Finish on each one–might be acceptable, but doing it for *a thousand* computers? Not so much. Even normal business processes like bringing on a new employee became a massive chore. In the old mainframe days, a new employee would get an account set up on the mainframe and a phone extension assigned to their desk, and that was pretty much it from a tech perspective. Now? New employees needed a user account, an email mailbox, a folder to store their documents in, access to the company applications, and more. Completing all those provisioning tasks manually could take hours, if not *days,* and organizations big and small started to feel the pain.

Simply put, Windows started to bog down in terms of the labor it required, and so computers running Linux started giving Microsoft trouble in enterprise environments.

Linux, an open-source operating system that's based on, and largely compatible with, Unix was created mainly in response to the high cost of Unix operating systems. Linux is free to use in most cases, and it runs on the same cheaper commodity hardware that Windows Server can run on. Linux is a lot harder to administer, though. It favors cryptic commands typed into the computer, versus Windows' pretty icons and Next-Next-Finish wizards. The upside of Linux is that once you *do* learn to manage it, it's almost as easy to manage a hundred computers as it is just one. Instead of typing the commands into each computer yourself, you simply type them into a text file not unlike a word-processing document, and tell all of your computers to run that text file. The text file becomes a "script," like you might hand out to actors in Hollywood, with each computer reading their lines so that you don't have to.

Microsoft started struggling to close deals in large companies due in part to the perception that managing large batches of Windows Server machines took more labor than doing the same thing with cheap Linux machines. Windows Server cost money too, and organizations didn't often see the point in spending a lot of money on something that was painstaking to administer and maintain.

Nowhere was Microsoft's problem more evident than in a leaked white paper from August 2000. This was shortly after Microsoft had acquired Hotmail, a free email service hosting more than 100 million accounts and running entirely on Unix servers running the

FreeBSD variant of Unix. Microsoft employees were tasked with performing an analysis of what it would take to move from Unix to Windows as the base of Hotmail, and the results weren't rosy.

"It's easy to look at a UNIX system," the paper's author says, "and know what is running and why. Although its configuration files may have arcane (and sometimes too-simple) syntax, they are easy to find and change." But with Windows, "Some parameters that control the system's operation are hidden and difficult to fully assess. The metabase is an obvious example. The problem here is that it makes the administrator nervous; in a single-function system he wants to be able to understand all of the configuration-related choices that the system is making on his behalf." And then a real strike against Windows, from a manageability perspective: "GUI operations are essentially impossible to script. With large numbers of servers, it is impractical to use the GUI to carry out installation tasks or regular maintenance tasks." For Unix? "Most configuration setups, log files, and so on, are plain text files with reasonably short line lengths. Although this may be marginally detrimental to performance (usually in circumstances where it doesn't matter) it is a powerful approach because a small, familiar set of tools, adapted to working with short text lines, can be used by the administrators for most of their daily tasks. In particular, favorite tools can be used to analyze all the system's log files and error reports."

The paper goes on to really lay out why Unix' approach was better: "Over the years, UNIX versions have evolved a good set of single-function commands and shell scripting languages that work well for ad-hoc and automated administration. The shell scripting languages fall just short of being a programming language (they have less power than VBScript or JScript). This may seem to be a disadvantage, but we must remember that operators are not programmers; having to learn a block-structured programming language is a resistance point." Furthermore, "PERL... is more of a programming than scripting language. It is popular for repeated, automated tasks that can be developed and optimized by senior administrative staff who do have the higher level of programming expertise required."

In other words: Windows was horrible at administrative automation, and VBScript wasn't helping. (As an aside, the Hotmail migration to Windows actually went off really well, with nobody realizing for months that the back-end migration had even happened.)

As the paper hints, Microsoft had first countered Unix' robust shell scripting history with Visual Basic Script, or VBScript. This scripting language was intended to let you manage Windows Server by typing commands into text files, just as Linux could do. But it was a programming language, not a shell scripting language. The barrier to entry for VBScript was high. You couldn't just run a command and then paste it into a script for long-term use; you had to *write code*. And the fundamental architecture of Windows Server wasn't the same as that of Linux, and it impacted Windows' ability to have an *effective* scripting language.

Linux, as with Unix before it, is a "text-based operating system." That's what the Hotmail white paper was alluding to: everything that tells the server how to behave–its *configuration*–is basically lines in text files. The operating system's means of communicating with other devices is similarly simplistic. Changing a text file is easy. Most Linux administrators quickly figured out the small number of tools that enabled them to change text files on hundreds of computers at once, effectively reconfiguring those computers with a single keystroke if needed. Sure, those tools were cryptic, with incomprehensible names like "grep," "sed," "awk," "cat," and more, but you only needed to learn them once. Once you did, the world of Linux administration was open to you. Learn a little, and you could do a lot.

Windows, on the other hand, is an API-based operating system. Each component inside Windows defines a set of interfaces that you use to tell it what to do. When you click an icon in Windows, one bit of software uses those interfaces to tell another bit of software to do something, like open a file, send a message, or whatever. Automating Windows administration, then, is less about changing text files and more about some pretty serious computer programming. These interfaces are (for the most part) documented, but that documentation presumes you're an experienced software engineer. Sadly, the people hired to manage computer networks tend not to be experienced software engineers. In the Windows world, they were used to clicking icons, not coding programs of a hundred lines or more. VBScript helped a *bit*, but VBScript couldn't access all of the APIs needed to make Windows do everything it did. Eventually, someone using VBScript would run into a situation they simply couldn't handle, leaving them to go back to clicking icons to make stuff happen.

Worse, Windows' various APIs had all been created by developers who never expected anyone but themselves to use those APIs. Some APIs required you to use low-level programming languages like C or C++, while others could use more accessible, higher-level languages like VBScript. Still others were best used from Microsoft's .NET Framework, a set of APIs released in the late 1990s to make software development faster and more consistent. But .NET Framework didn't cover everything a server administrator might need. So this wasn't just a matter of Windows being based on APIs; it was also about Microsoft having changed their minds over the years on how those APIs were created and used. You could be a master in .NET Framework, for example, and still be unable to deal with some of the deeper, C++-based interfaces in Windows' core.

Lest you think Microsoft had been remiss in their architecture, rest assured that's not the case. Using APIs to wall off different components from each other is not only a standard practice, it's a *recommended* practice. APIs let multiple teams of people work on different subsystems without interference or dependencies on other teams. One team can do whatever they like with their piece of software, knowing that all they need to do is publish an interface through which other teams could access whatever was needed. It's a bit like the radio in your car: you might not know how a radio works, but you can use the interface provided to change stations and adjust the volume. The back side of the radio sports another interface that lets the car supply power, antenna signals, and so on to the radio. If you buy a Ford truck, you're welcome to swap out the Ford radio for a Pioneer one, provided the Pioneer radio can support the same interface that your truck expects of a radio (which is why adapter cables exist).

A problem with interfaces, though, is that they can only give you the things their developer anticipated you would need. If your truck radio has no interface for taking a satellite radio signal, then there's nothing you can do about that, no matter how many adapter cables you have. And that's where Windows administrators often found themselves: if the developers of some Windows subsystem hadn't *anticipated* an administrator needing to do something, then the subsystem's interfaces wouldn't make it possible, and the administrator was out of luck.

And here's another problem Windows had: many of the teams who built Windows' various components assumed nobody would ever do anything other than click the pretty icons they'd created. For those components, it was essentially impossible to automate their administration because they simply had no interfaces through which to do so. It was, frankly, a bit of a mess, and it caused no end of frustration to Windows administrators who were managing a rapidly growing number of servers in their environments. This wasn't necessarily a bad decision on the part of those teams, because the *whole point* of Windows was its graphical user interface. For many of them, suggesting that people might need to administer using something other than icons and wizards approached heresy. Teams were *required* to deliver a comprehensive and easy-to-use graphical user interface. Anything else was often optional in terms of Microsoft's architecture standards, and optional things tend to fall by the wayside when resources get tight and timelines get short.

Linux, to be clear, also *technically* relies on APIs. It's just that nearly every piece of Linux adopted "put stuff in text files" as their interface. If you want to reconfigure a piece of Windows–say, you need to add a user account to the company directory–you have to hope the directory subsystem's APIs offer a way to do that, and then you have to learn what data structure to pass them to make them do it. With Linux, you often just add a line to a text file. Notably, many recent Microsoft products have shifted to this text-based approach. With Microsoft Azure, for example, a specially formatted text file can be used to make Azure do almost anything.

But in the early- to mid-2000s, complex APIs still ruled Windows Server. It seemed like all the bits were there to automate *most* Windows administration, but they were scattered over a half dozen largely difficult and sometimes-incompatible languages and technologies. It's like going into an auto shop and realizing you need a set of metric sockets for the frame of the vehicle, Imperial sockets for the body, a torch welder for the roof, and a magic wand for the engine. If you can master *all* of the different tools then maybe you're fine, but it's a lot to wrap your head around.

This problem would have been solvable: you just need your Windows server administrators to be *really* broad in terms of the technologies they can support, and *really* fast at learning new things. Basically, if your admins are capable of being ersatz developers, you're fine. Except that wasn't the sales pitch Microsoft had been making for a decade. "Administer your network as easily as you use your own desktop!" had been the message, not "Learn four programming languages and spend all your time writing code!" The bulk of Microsoft's administrator audience wasn't up to speed on software programming, and in a lot of cases they weren't *interested* in learning languages like C#, C++, VBScript, or whatever else. Again, it's as if Microsoft had attracted a large audience of competent, intelligent, hardworking automotive mechanics, and then carried a nuclear reactor into the shop and said, "You can do this too, right?" The audience was used to a certain level of consistency and abstraction that a graphical user interface affords, and they simply hadn't been prepared to have Windows' underlying inconsistencies and ugliness dumped in their laps.

Understand, too, that in 2003, Windows administrators tended to be paid markedly less than software developers with equivalent seniority, and in many cases less than similarly situated Linux or Unix administrators. The assumption that "managing Windows is easy!" was baked into their salaries, and the idea of suddenly being asked to take on a very different kind of role, without necessarily being paid more, didn't sit well.

This is the world that PowerShell (originally *Windows* PowerShell) was born into: Windows Server struggling to compete with Linux in large-scale companies, due in main part to the relative difficulty in automating Windows administration at scale. Under the hood, Windows was a hodgepodge of different interconnected systems, each one optimized for whatever its task was, and each one difficult to automate without knowing a half dozen or more different technologies and approaches.

The thing is, Microsoft had known this was a problem for quite a while, and their initial solution wasn't even aimed at Windows administrators.

Illustrating the Problem

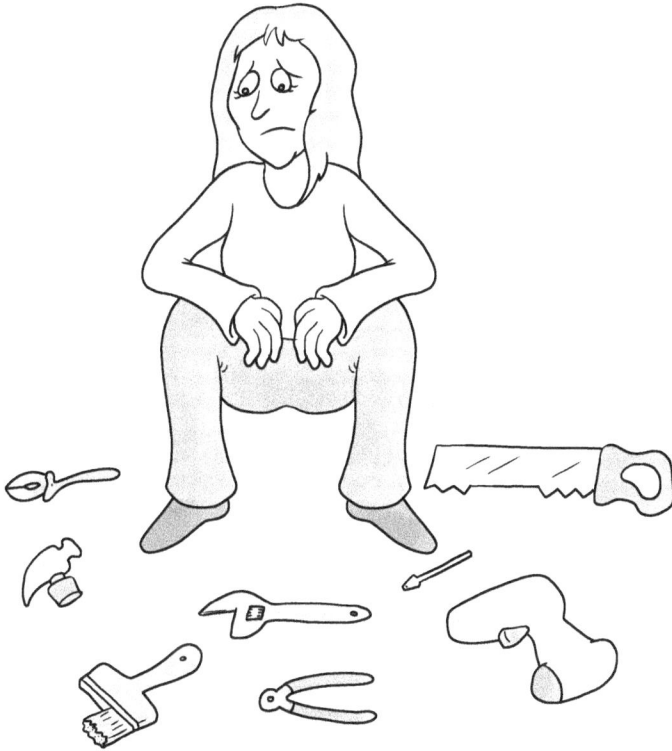

Take the seemingly simple problem of adding a new user to a Microsoft Active Directory domain, a task that most large companies must perform several times each day.

Microsoft's first-class citizen approach was to use the Active Directory Users and Computers graphical user interface, or GUI. ADUC, as it's often called, was created as a "snap-in," or extension, to a generic GUI administration tool called the Microsoft Management

Console, or MMC. The idea with the MMC was to provide administrators with a single window–a "single pane of glass," in industry parlance–where they could do anything their jobs needed. Need to administer your company's Domain Name System? Add the DNS snap-in to the MMC. Need to do something with the Microsoft SQL Server? Add the right snap-in to the MMC. The MMC was part of Microsoft's "Common Engineering Criteria," or CEC, of the day, and it was an attempt to make all of the company's various GUI administration consoles more accessible and more consistent.

But you still had to click icons. A large company that brought on a dozen new employees or more every day could easily wind up with one or more human beings who literally did nothing but click buttons and checkboxes in the ADUC GUI. Many organizations rightfully saw that as a waste of human labor and looked for automation solutions.

But as we've learned, Microsoft was leagues away from having a cohesive automation story. In this instance, an administrator looking to automate Active Directory user creation might have to explore no less than *eleven* potential tools to see if any of them could get the job done:

- The Active Directory Services Interface (ADSI) Windows NT (WinNT), provider
- The ADSI Lightweight Directory Access Protocol (LDAP) provider–similar to its WinNT sibling, but with distinct capabilities
- Using a Csvde.exe command-line tool to import a comma-separated values file containing the new user data
- Running the Dsadd.exe command-line tool
- Using the LDAP Data Interchange Format (Ldifde.exe) tool
- Using a .NET Framework class–there were several potential ones to choose from–in a program
- Using Windows Management Instrumentation (WMI).

None of these tools accomplished exactly the same thing, although they all had overlap with each other. If you were creating a simple user account–a name and a password, perhaps–any of them might have done the trick. But companies also tend to log data like an employee's department, manager name, address, phone extension, and so on, and only *some* of those tools could do all of those. Still other attributes in Active Directory were accessible *only* from the GUI, so many administrators would spend days or weeks experimenting with various tools only to glumly return to the GUI after failing to find an automation tool that could do everything they needed.

The underlying reasons for all this were mainly political, and they were legion.

Microsoft product teams are largely autonomous, and often smaller than outsiders imagine. Although shipped as part of the Microsoft Windows Server operating system, Active Directory is its own product team, distinct from the base operating system. Teams– at least back then–tended to operate as self-contained fiefdoms, cooperating with other teams only at need, and typically only when sufficient political capital existed to compel cooperation.

Within the Windows operating system universe, including its many sub-components like Active Directory, the Common Engineering Criteria was one of the few documents that provided cross-team requirements. If the CEC said you had to provide administrative capabilities by means of an MMC snap-in then you *had* to do it, even if taking the time to do so meant sidelining some other features you'd hoped to work into your next release. Notably, the CEC in 2003 didn't touch on administrative automation at all, so it's no wonder so few Microsoft products of the time got automation right. Even when the teams *knew* they had an automation problem, they often didn't have the time or budget to address it.

A team was welcome to provide capabilities above and beyond the CEC, if they had the resources to do so. The automation tools produced by the Active Directory team tended to focus on bulk import of users, because those bulk imports were a key scenario in migrating large enterprise customers from a competing solution. Enabling migration meant winning deals, which meant incoming revenue, so it's hardly surprising that those scenarios were the ones prioritized over automating day-to-day administration. Few technology executives of the time were sophisticated enough to consider "how will we manage this thing day-to-day" in their purchasing decisions, and–again, at the time–the ones who were tended to avoid Windows when they could.

It's worth noting that writing automation tooling isn't easy, which is another reason why few Microsoft teams committed to it. Developing an MMC snap-in *was* relatively easy: the MMC itself provided a lot of the code that was boring, such as presenting different views for data, intercepting user clicks and interpreting them as actions, and so on. The MMC was kind of a framework of functionality that was common to GUI-based administration, and so knocking out an MMC snap-in, while not trivial, wasn't a huge investment.

Nothing like the MMC existed for automation-enabled tools, though. Teams looking to create command-line tools, which could be more easily integrated into scripts, were *entirely* on their own. They had to develop their own command structure, write code to accept and interpret commands, develop output displays, and more. It's actually a *lot* of work, and given the competing priorities of the day–and the fact that the MMC was a CEC requirement–many teams simply couldn't afford the investment.

To get really specific, imagine that you're on a product team that handles Windows' Dynamic Host Configuration Protocol, or DHCP. DHCP is designed to automatically issue, track, and manage the addresses that computers need in order to participate on a network (your home WiFi router, for example, usually includes DHCP functionality so that your smart phone, laptop, and smart TV can all get on the network). In enterprise environments, critical computers like servers often have a manually created reservation for their address so they get the same one every time they connect to the network. As a product team, let's say you've been interviewing customers and have figured out that the ability to bulk-manage reservations is really important to them. So you sit down to design a tool called "dhcpmanage." You come up with a few use cases:

- Customers might create a comma-separated values, or CSV, file in Excel that lists the reservations they want to create, and then import it by running dhcpmanage -file reservations.csv.
- Customers might want the tool to create a CSV file of existing reservations, and they might run dhcpmanage -export current.csv.
- The tool might also need to add or remove existing reservations one at a time, perhaps by running dhcpmanage -add 192.168.13.12 -for 00:D3:32:EE:12:34:56:78, or dhcpmanage -remove 00:D3:32:EE:12:34:56:78.

Let's say that's as far as you decide to go in your tool's initial release. Your team has a *lot* of work ahead of it! In addition to coding the basic functionality to add or remove reservations, you have to:

- Code the ability to read files
- Code the ability to write files
- Ensure your code can deal with an improperly formatted file or other error condition
- Write a parser that looks at what the user types and figures out which task they're trying to do
- Ensure any messages or errors your tool displays can be displayed in whatever language the computer is set to (Microsoft is a global company, and almost all tools have some level of localization)
- Run all of your code through testing to ensure it works

It's a lot of work. Even a tool of that simplicity may require a few hundred person-hours by the time it's designed, coded, tested, and made ready to ship. And the annoying part is that the work is more or less one-off, meaning that if another team needed to write a tool for *their* product, there's very little work they can leverage from other teams. Every tool is a new, start-from-scratch experience. That gets expensive.

The go-it-on-your-own approach to Microsoft product teams didn't help, either. With no framework for command-line tools in place at the operating system level, and with each team basically choosing their own destiny when it came to what they produced, the tools that *did* get produced were all but incompatible with each other. One team might produce a great command-line tool that could grab user information from a Human Resources database, but there might not be any way to link that data to a tool that could create new Active Directory user accounts. The walls between the tools reflected the political boundaries between teams.

Those walls and inconsistencies often proved to be a disincentive for Microsoft's customers. When every tool was unique, might not do *everything* the customer needed, might not play well with the other tools the customer was already using... well, a lot of customers just ignored what tools there were, because using them was more effort than it was worth. When the tools didn't get used, the product teams had a disincentive to make more tools, and so the problem just cycled and got worse.

As we've seen, it was a mess. But Unix wasn't a mess, right? So let's just copy that!

Let's Just Copy Unix

A common refrain amongst Microsoft's bigger critics was, "Why don't you just do what Unix does?" Unix, after all, was thriving in enterprises, and offered a rich set of command-line tools that enabled pretty much any kind of automation you could think of. And of course the same applied to Unix' open-source offspring, Linux.

But as we've discussed, Unix and Windows are very different kinds of operating systems. What works for Unix won't automatically work for Windows; the two operating systems take radically different approaches to how they work, let alone how you administer them.

And let's be honest for a moment: Unix' command-line administration isn't exactly a piece of fine art. Yes, once you comprehend it, you can get the job done, and done well, but coming to comprehend it is a *huge* task.

Unix gets a lot of things right when it comes to the command-line: most of its tools are fairly atomic, which means they tend to do one thing and do that one thing well. You get one tool to change the owner of a file and another to change the permissions on the file. Atomicity is a good thing because it makes tools simpler to write and use, and makes them usable in a broader set of scenarios when an administrator is orchestrating several tools to act together.

But figuring out which Unix tool to use for a given task–heck, even figuring out what tools *exist* from the thousands that are out there– is really, really hard. Linux probably never would have taken off the way it did if it hadn't been for Google's ability to help new administrators figure out whether grep, sed, awk, or something else was the right tool for the job at hand. Prior to Google, you could walk by most Unix administrators' desks and find thick books containing command reference material.

And administrators needed that reference material, because learning to use one tool gave you almost no advantage when it came to learning other tools. One tool might require you to type -m to specify the name of a remote machine while another might want you to use -Comp or -n or \c or --computer for the same purpose. There was precious little consistency between the more than 3,300 command-line tools that existed in Red Hat Enterprise Linux, or RHEL, circa 2003, making each tool a unique and challenging experience for a new administrator.

Unix' tools–like the operating system itself–were text-based. That means that when you ran a tool, whatever it produced was displayed on-screen as text. It's entirely possible to pass that text to another tool, which forms the foundation of automation, but it took a lot of work. For example, suppose you had a tool that could retrieve usernames from a database and another tool that could set up email accounts for those users. The first tool might list the username in the second on-screen column of data, occupying character positions 10 through 20, say. You'd have to pass, or "pipe," that data to a middleman tool that could extract just columns 10-20 before piping the result on to the email account tool. This kind of text parsing was part and parcel of every Unix admin's day-to-day life. And it was brittle: if the first tool's author revised it and moved the name information to columns 12-22, then everything you'd written would break and you'd have to go fix it all. As a result, tools were rarely revised in that way. Instead, a tool's author might just add a switch to change the output to a different format, giving you something *more* to learn and requiring that the author continue to support decades-old ways of doing things, just because changing it would probably break something else.

So Unix and Linux had some good things going for them, but they also had a lot of inconsistent, difficult cruft that had built up over the years, much of which it inherited from their decades-old Unix predecessors.

But sometimes it's actually easier just to reproduce the cruft that already exists than to think of something entirely new and better. Sometimes, "Just let us do what we've always been able to do," is all the mission calls for. Microsoft's next-generation shell *could* have simply been a faithful recreation of what had worked for so long on Unix.

In fact, it almost was *exactly* that.

Kermit

In the early 2000s, Intel–the world's largest producer of microprocessors and the biggest player in the PC architecture that most copies of Microsoft Windows ran on–had a bit of an embarrassing secret. Although Intel was famous for their Complex Instruction Set Computing, or CISC, processors, those chips were designed on a competing technology. Intel owns thousands of Sun Microsystems SPARC workstations that are based on Reduced Instruction Set

Computing, or RISC, chips and running Sun's Unix-variant operating system, Solaris. Intel wasn't thrilled with the fact that their
own chips weren't powerful enough to design their next generation,
and so CEO Craig Barrett started talking to Microsoft's Bill Gates
about it.

The plan was to migrate Intel entirely to an Intel-based chip design
platform, but more powerful chips couldn't provide the complete
solution. Computers need powerful hardware, but they also need
software, in the form of an operating system, that can fully leverage
that hardware. Gates agreed to make the changes necessary to Windows to enable Intel's migration, and started dedicating resources
inside Microsoft toward making it happen.

Nobody at Microsoft knew, of course, that Intel had already started
a parallel effort to migrate their workstations to Intel-based machines running a Linux variant. Ultimately, Microsoft's efforts
wouldn't achieve what they'd originally envisioned, but this is
where the seed of PowerShell came into existence.

Windows NT had been designed to run multiple "subsystems,"
each essentially a mini operating system. The theory–never fully
brought to reality, but a good theory nonetheless–was to enable
Windows as a kind of super-operating system to run applications
written for other operating systems. The Win32 subsystem would
run Windows-native applications, a POSIX subsystem would provide basic Unix compatibility, an OS/2 subsystem would run IBM
OS/2 applications, and so on. Windows integrated a "Services
for Unix" application suite, which provided key interoperability
mechanisms that let Windows play nicely on a Unix network.

Intel's biggest concerns for Windows boiled down to one main
thing: a robust command-line shell, just as they had on their SPARC
workstations. Ideally, they wanted a Unix shell that could run all
the scripts and tools they'd already built for themselves. And so one
of the teams Gates had funded within Microsoft was tasked with
making it happen. Daryl Wray, a Program Manager in Microsoft at

the time, proposed to create an implementation of a popular Unix shell, KornShell, or ksh, to run on Windows, and he nicknamed his project "Kermit." Not after the famous frog Muppet, but after *Kermit the Hermit,* a children's book by Bill Peet about a crab. Crabs live in shells, you see, and Wray and team were setting out to create a new shell.

Wray's team wasn't trying to be overly ambitious, and they weren't trying to change the world. Implementing KornShell on Windows would simply let Intel's team run the command-line utilities that they were used to running. It was an eminently practical solution to the problem: "What is it you really need to do?" "Run these tools." "Okay, we'll make that happen."

Wray came from the Unix world and understood how Unix administrators worked. He understood their hard-won expertise with command-line stalwarts like `grep`, `sed`, and `awk`, and he understood how brittle Unix scripts could be. Moving a Unix script from one variant of Unix to another would almost always cause problems and require rewriting because the tools on different variants weren't always 100% consistent. The decision to port KornShell was made primarily because it lined up with what Intel's engineers were already doing and would ensure the least amount of breakage during a migration.

The Kermit effort lived within the Windows Client team in Microsoft. At the time, Windows Client and Server were considered distinct operating systems with some shared components. Because Kermit was intended to address a client-side issue, namely the existence of a command-line shell on chip design workstations, it was owned by the Client team. That would create some friction in the future, but for right now Kermit had two things going for it.

First, Kermit was a funded project with a team of around a dozen people. That's important, because putting together a team within Microsoft was always challenging, requiring business justifications, funding, and more. Those things were now out of the way.

Second, a Microsoft architect named Jeffrey Snover had caught wind of Kermit, and had big ideas for it.

A Manifesto

Jeffrey Snover came to Microsoft's world at Digital Equipment Cor-poration, or DEC, where he was, in his words, "the shortest-lived consulting engineer in the company." Snover had been brought in to work on a product called NetView, which was DEC's version of OpenView, a cross-platform management tool. Specifically, Snover had been asked to help port NetView to Windows because DEC didn't have a strong Windows presence at the time. But Snover didn't realize that DEC was about to sell almost all of its software applications to Computer Associates, also known simply as CA. Then a strange thing happened: it turned out that NetView was jointly owned by DEC and IBM, so DEC wasn't permitted to sell it to CA. DEC had to draw up a list of which assets were considered part of NetView, and which weren't; the ones that weren't would be sold to CA. Snover's name was at the top of the list of non-NetView assets, meaning he'd be shipped to CA.

Snover wasn't thrilled. CA is often referred to as the company "where good software goes to die;" it's acquisition-heavy, and not universally known as a great place to work. Snover wasn't interested in working for them, but he knew that IBM had recently acquired another cross-platform monitoring and management solution known as Tivoli. Before the CA deal could close, he reached out to IBM and made the case that they should hire him, which they did. IBM didn't care a lot about Windows back then, but Tivoli had a pretty good Windows story and so it seemed like a good fit.

It makes sense that once Snover was ready to leave Tivoli he'd not only go to Microsoft but also wind up as an architect in charge of various management and monitoring efforts within the company.

Snover joined Microsoft as a Chief Architect in the Windows Platform team, and was tasked with improving the overall manageability of the Windows platform. He pressed for command-line scripting as the answer, and was finally given some budget to hire a bunch of contractors to write a batch of typical, standalone commands. The idea was to increase the number of commands administrators had to work with, and thereby start slowly chipping away at the difficulty of managing Windows from a command-line. His initial budget was a few million dollars, and he was able to produce 40 commands from that.

Forty commands for a few million dollars. Suddenly, the task of making Windows more automation-friendly was starting to look like an impossibly high mountain. If Windows ultimately needed *hundreds* of commands, how many millions of dollars–and how many years–would the company have to invest?

The problem was one you've already learned about: in addition to writing the code needed to make the command do its thing, each command had to be designed. Each command needed a parser to figure out what the user was asking it to do. Each command needed to deal with error conditions and display appropriate messages. Each command had to figure out how to display its output. Snover's contractors were all doing a lot of the same work, but couldn't really share a lot of code because each effort was unique to each command.

Around the same time, Snover started looking hard at Windows Management Instrumentation. Designed as a Windows-specific implementation of the industry-wide and vendor-neutral Common Information Model, or CIM, WMI, as everyone called it, seemed to hold a lot of promise. WMI was built around an extensible repository
model. Essentially, developers could write a WMI "provider" that would populate the repository with management information. Some providers could even accept changes from the repository and use those to reconfigure the computer. WMI had a number of internal champions at Microsoft, and those champions had been pretty successful in getting Microsoft's various product teams to write WMI providers for their products. In theory, the WMI repository was a rich resource of management information. Providers existed for the core operating system, the base computer hardware, for products like DNS and Active Directory, and so on. Since teams had already done the work to create those providers, the WMI repository should have been a great way for administrators to be more effective.

The problem was that almost nobody was *using* WMI at any kind of scale. That's because the champions who'd been pressing for product teams to support WMI hadn't been promulgating many standards or best practices. The repository's contents were poorly documented and difficult to browse, so nobody really knew what was in it. Different providers worked a bit differently, which made them all a bit confusing to use. There weren't even any straightforward tools that let an administrator access WMI; most administrators touched WMI by means of VBScript, which tended to require a lot of programming.

But where others saw confusion and complexity, Snover saw an opportunity. He designed a command called WMIC, which was in reality an engine of sorts: a generic command that could adapt as it went, designed to make the WMI repository easier to work with, more consistent, and more discoverable. The idea was that WMIC could take an easy-to-produce metadata file that told the engine how to work with a particular piece of the repository. Writing metadata files was a very low incremental investment; over one Christmas break, Snover himself wrote metadata files for a whole slew of commands to prove the concept. A mere $40,000 investment got Microsoft the WMIC engine *and* 72 additional cmdlets (pronounced "command-lets")–a far better return on investment than spending millions of dollars for 40 commands! Another $100,000 investment added sorting, filtering, list and table formatting, and other tools to WMIC. "We've got some juice here!" Snover realized.

WMI itself was an object-oriented system. When you queried management information from the repository–say, asking it to return information about the basic computer system hardware–you got back a set of objects. These objects had properties that described the hardware, and methods that enabled you to make changes to the configuration. WMIC worked directly with those objects, effectively making it the first object-oriented shell–although it was a very limited shell compared to the shells of operating systems like Linux or Unix. But getting WMIC to where it was opened Snover's eyes to some of the architectural possibilities.

33

A third round of WMIC funding was aimed at adding XSL processing and XSL transformations, or XSLTs. In essence, an XSL file is an XML-formatted file that provides a template of sorts for displaying data. An XSLT takes a data set and a specified template and transforms the data set. The idea was very powerful, but in terms of a practical implementation it didn't really go anywhere. However, it did demonstrate the potential of an XSLT pipeline, and during the course of development it demonstrated how Microsoft's fairly new .NET Framework made it pretty easy to work with XML data and object-based structures. *That* would become crucial to PowerShell's existence. And it didn't hurt that Bill Gates, still in charge of the company at the time, was trumpeting .NET Framework from the figurative rooftops and encouraging everyone to use it.

That's around when Snover got wind of the Kermit project and saw an opportunity. He pitched his boss the idea of an object-oriented shell based on an engine and powered by cmdlets.

He was told no.

"Well, I've done this prototype," he said, "and I think this is the best idea. There's this other team doing a shell, and I'm going to change groups to go with this."

"If you change groups," he was warned, "I'll demote you. You have a performance problem, and if you leave the group, you'll get dropped two levels. But if you stay here you won't get demoted!"

"This was the first I'd heard that I had a performance problem," Snover said later, "and I certainly didn't understand why, if I have a problem, I wouldn't get demoted just by staying." So he spoke to the manager of the other team and explained the problem. They agreed that Snover would change teams and get the work underway. Then, they'd evaluate his performance and make a decision about his job level. In the end, his new position wound up being one step down, mainly because his job scope simply couldn't justify his original pay level. It's all worked out in the end, as Snover is now a Technical Fellow, Microsoft's highest-ranked (and most rare) technical leader position.

So Snover more or less co-opted the old Kermit team and recruited several additional individuals from within Microsoft. Jim Truher and Bruce Payette joined from the Services for Unix team, Bruce in particular bringing a wealth of language design experience. Kenneth Hansen had been leading a provisioning product that relied heavily on XML, making him seem like a good fit for the new shell's program management team. Lee Holmes found PowerShell internally and started giving great feedback, leading to a lunch with Snover and an eventual move to the team, and brought a greatly transformed security story to the shell.

Snover had seen what Kermit was meant to achieve, and he had his WMIC experience behind him. It seemed like a perfect combination: take this existing team that's trying to build a shell, take the idea for an object-oriented, .NET-based shell that had come from his WMIC work, and put the two together.

It took some doing, but people were intrigued.

At the time, Microsoft had some strong advocates for using the company's India Development Center, or IDC, on software development projects. Specifically, S. Somasegar, head of Microsoft's Developer Division (DevDiv, which owns the Visual Studio product line amongst other things), was happy to find budget for projects that were using the IDC. Jim Allchin, the leader of Microsoft's Platforms Division at the time, wanted a command-line shell. *Any* shell. Snover agreed: he'd develop Allchin's shell, and he'd use the IDC to do it. So development got underway.

Or it tried to get underway.

There were numerous problems with using the IDC, it turned out. The developers and engineers there were smart, but they were twelve and a half time zones away from Redmond, Washington.

That meant questions wound up having a 24-hour turnaround time, as the teams in India and the US were essentially working opposite shifts. Snover even spent weeks waking up early and staying up late, specifically to try and shorten the question-and-answer turnaround time. And the questions were *numerous,* as nobody in the IDC was familiar with Windows administration, scripting, and so on.

Snover decided to try and put together a "vision and mission" document. Something concise that would enable the IDC developers to work more independently, and to make decisions that would lead toward the stated vision. He knew he needed a strong vision of what his new solution would be. He needed something concise, clear, and passionate that others could rally around. A long-term vision, one that, in totality, solved the various problems with Windows administration that he'd identified. The result was the Monad Manifesto[5].

The *Monad Manifesto* laid out Snover's vision. It begins with a concise statement of the problem: administrators need to be able to automate server administration, and Windows' existing approaches are inconsistent, incomplete, and less approachable to the typical administrator.

The manifesto then lays out four steps toward solving the problem. Step one, Snover wrote, was a shell that enabled "composable commands." Notably, this was a Unix- or Linux-style "text shell" where administrators would type commands, rather than a "graphical shell" where people clicked icons. Text shells invariably lead to scripting, and scripting invariably leads to large-scale automation, which was the whole point of the thing. But Snover's vision specifically didn't end with a text shell: he wanted a shell with commands that could connect to each other to perform complex tasks. A shell whose commands had sensible names, like "Get Content," rather than obscure, nerd-friendly names like "cat."

Step two was a shell that could communicate with copies of itself

---

[5]https://leanpub.com/themonadmanifestoannotated

on remote computers, enabling scenarios where administrators could connect to and configure multiple computers with a single command.

Step three was a shell that could run complex scripts that involved numerous steps, might need to run over a long period of time, and might need to keep running even if the computer restarted.

Step four was a shell that could accept a definition of how a computer *should* be configured, and then configure the computer to match that, and keep it that way, automatically.

It was a big vision. So big, in fact, that nothing existed at the time that actually accomplished *all* of those things. Not on Windows, not on Linux, not on Unix. This was true first principle thinking: ignoring what had come before and focusing on what was needed. For most administrators at the time, merely completing step one would have been enough, and step two felt like a dream come true. The functionality promised by steps three and four was so innovative at the time that many people didn't even pay attention to them.

To be sure, PowerShell would eventually take inspiration from a number of predecessors, but its goals began as ambitious, as-pirational statements grounded in what Snover saw the world needing, much of which hadn't existed up to that point. But over the course of its first four versions, PowerShell would accomplish–with varying degrees of success and adoption–all of the goals Snover outlined in his *Manifesto*.

But it's not enough to simply write a manifesto. Having a vision is a very different thing from bringing that vision to life, especially inside a company that had made its name by organizing systems administration around cute, clickable graphic icons.

In the end, the Manifesto wasn't enough to keep the IDC team moving at speed. The slow pace of the work effort, the constant back-and-forth, and the core misunderstandings of what "scripting" meant, was dragging the project down. The IDC team was shifted to other work, and Snover and the remaining US team began the hard work of building a new team almost from scratch.

Jeffrey Snover is something of a Renaissance man. He may be a Technical Fellow for one of the world's largest technology companies, but he's just as happy to dive into esoteric philosophy, discuss why concrete is humankind's greatest invention, or haul out some obscure fact. He's *great* at cocktail parties, and thanks to his Boston upbringing, he curses inventively and frequently, bringing a great deal of color to his stories.

The term "monad," from the Greek word *monas*, refers, in cosmogony, to the Supreme Being, divinity, or the totality of all things. Philosophically, it refers to a single source acting alone, to an "indivisible origin," or to something that embodies both. That concept was adopted by other, later philosophers, such as Leibniz, who referred to the monad as an *elementary particle*.

Gottfried Wilhelm von Leibniz was a prominent German polymath and logician in the early 1700s. He was also a philosopher noted for his optimism, or his conclusion that our universe is the best possible one that could have been created. That universe, he proposed, was composed of *monads*, an infinite number of simple substances. What we experience as our universe is simply those monads arranged in different compositions. Each monad, in Leibniz' philosophy, follows a pre-programmed set of instructions that are unique to itself, so that it knows what to do at any given moment.

You can see why the term was appealing to Snover as he contemplated his new shell: each cmdlet would be a monad of sorts, and by composing them in different sequences, administrators could perform and automate whatever tasks they needed.

Culture

To really understand PowerShell's history and some of the design decisions its creators made, you have to understand a bit about the culture of early-2000s Microsoft under then-CEO Steve Ballmer.

At the time, Microsoft was purely a Waterfall software development company. "Waterfall" is a sort of project management approach that's used for creating software, and it had been successfully used for decades. At its most basic, Waterfall dictates that you exhaustively research the problem your software will try to solve, gathering every possible requirement and *completely* understanding the problem space. Then, you create a set of specification documents that describe exactly what the software will do and how it will do it. With all that in hand, you then begin a series of development cycles that might last *years* to create the software itself. During those cycles, software developers create code. They ship that code to testers, often on a nightly basis, and the testers run the code through exhaustive batteries of manual and automated tests. Once all the code is done, and all the tests are passed, your software is ready for release.

Companies are finite things, meaning they always have limitations. As it turns out, *writing* code as a software developer is far, far, far easier than *testing* that code. A single software developer might spend an eight-hour workday churning out code on a computer. To test that code, along with all the code it relies on and affects, might require a 16-hour overnight shift involving dozens and dozens of computers and multiple test specialists.

At Microsoft, and most especially within the Windows Server teams, *no code leaves the building until it's been tested.* Period. Windows ships to *billions* of computers on the planet, and Microsoft's customers expect stable, high-performance, reliable code. Testing is important.

But that requirement creates a lot of problems when you're trying to churn out a *lot* of code, because while it might be easy (or at least straightforward) to actually code it, getting it through test might be hard. Microsoft's archives are *filled* with code for great software that simply couldn't get prioritized for testing, and was therefore never released.

Microsoft's software development culture of the time created two unique problems for Jeffrey Snover as PowerShell development moved from the India Development Center to Microsoft's campus in Redmond, Washington.

First, he was now dealing with developers who had come from the Windows Server team. Every software engineer needed to know the complete story up front. "The problem was," Snover recalls, "you *couldn't.* Some of what we were doing hadn't ever been done. We needed to *do* some of it to figure out what the next bit would be, but they wouldn't write a single line of code–literally, not one line–until they knew the complete story." He eventually had to go to management and threaten to write the whole thing himself, at which point they pulled the trigger and got coding underway. Coding... but not necessarily testing.

It's worth mentioning that nobody on the PowerShell team, least of all Snover, had any objection to testing code. The objection was more about the *way* Microsoft tested code.

When Snover came to Microsoft from Tivoli, he came from an environment where developers were responsible for their code quality. Unit tests, which are small tests usually written by the developer and then run in an automated fashion, were a big thing. They enabled a developer to write some code and immediately run a series of automated tests to make sure their code was doing what it was supposed to do. Once all the tests passed, you knew you'd hit the level of code quality you were aiming for. Unit testing is itself a bit of an art, and teams that really master it can pump out demonstrably higher quality code.

But the Microsoft of the early 2000s had a different approach. Developers would write code–likely performing some informal testing as they went, of course–and then toss it over the wall to the testing group. It could be months, or even weeks, before that code would get tested, by which point the original developer would have moved on to something else or potentially even left the team or the company.

Snover had never before worked in a place where testing was handled that way, and where code quality was owned by someone other than the developers. His opinion was that having developers own their code created better code than what Microsoft was delivering at the time, and so he wanted PowerShell to take a different path than most Microsoft products of the time. He made a requirement that PowerShell's code be unit-tested every step of the way.

The developers from a non-Windows background–Jim Truher, Bruce Payette, and so on–were all for it. The more traditional-Microsoft developers, on the other hand, pushed back hard. Testing, those developers felt, was beneath them; testing was something given to junior people who couldn't "make it" as a "real" developer. But Snover held firm, refusing to budge on his unit-testing requirement. Again, the developers pushed back, saying they'd be less productive if they had to write code *and* write unit tests for it. Snover disagreed, insisting they would be *more* productive. They said he was crazy.

He insisted some more.

As coding began, Snover saw more and more code check-ins with no unit tests, and so he confronted the team. "We don't have time right now," they said. "We'll write the tests at the end of the release, and run them all then."

"You'll write them now," Snover said. Another battle ensued, and Snover won again. Code check-ins started coming in with unit tests, but also with bugs. So Snover dug into the code, and saw that the unit tests had been written, but not run. Another battle kicked off to make everyone actually run the tests.

You start to get a sense for how much Microsoft developers of that time *hated* testing and code quality.

The next battle was, "No, you have to *write* the tests, you have to *run* the tests, and you can't check in your code unless *all* the tests have passed. 'Some' is not enough. 'Most' is not enough."

Then it was, "No, *all* the tests have to pass. Everyone's, not just yours."

Eventually, Snover's admitted bullheadedness on the issue won through, and everyone was writing and running unit tests on their code. "You know what?" one of the more resistant developers finally told Snover, "We've been able to run the nightly build every day for the last couple of months. We've never been able to do that with any other project and it's because of the unit tests." The developer thanked Snover for his stubbornness on the issue.

Indeed, PowerShell versions have almost always shipped with a ridiculously low number of critical bugs, and low numbers of less-critical bugs. Snover attributes that to unit testing, something the world of software development today actually takes for granted.

PowerShell's architecture—which was similar to WMIC in that it consisted first of an abstract engine—was also a tactical decision intended to overcome Microsoft's culture. Remember, the PowerShell engine itself doesn't *do* anything. It simply provides a framework in which other things can run, and provides shared resources like a command parser, a help system, a formatting system, and so on. But by focusing on just the engine, *only the engine needed to get through testing.* Because the engine itself was the only code being shipped, it was the only thing that would need to get through the agonizing testing process. The actual cmdlets that would run *in* the engine could, Snover reasoned, be "shipped out of band." That is, they could be posted as source code to blogs, created and distributed outside Microsoft, and so on. Microsoft, as a company, would focus on the core value of the engine as their deliverable.

Focusing on the engine solved another problem. Snover knew that for PowerShell to be successful, it would have to be embraced by Microsoft's various product teams: SQL Server, Exchange Server, System Center, SharePoint, you name it. Those teams were already running hard and fast, and rarely had a ton of bandwidth to take on new projects. Many had already committed to WMI but seen very little return on that investment because of WMI's eccentricities (and WMIC had, in the end, not made a major positive impact on that). They'd be reluctant to commit to something new that alleged to solve the same problems.

And if they *did* commit, Snover knew they'd all head off in their own direction. Each team would concoct a different command vocabulary. They'd all write their own, inconsistent parsers. They'd use different syntax. They'd all approach output formatting differently. And anything they wrote would have to make it through testing, which would artificially bottleneck how much they could produce!

So PowerShell's engine would do all of the common heavy lifting: formatting, parsing, vocabulary definition, syntax definition, and so on. Product teams' cmdlets would be absolutely minimal, which would make them both easier to write *and* easier to test. More teams would be willing to invest, and the end results would be more consistent, creating a win for PowerShell's audience of administrators.

It was a brilliant architectural workaround to a distinct cultural problem (one that Microsoft largely does not have today), but it created problems of its own.

The .NET Framework Connection

To fully understand PowerShell and some of its earliest challenges, you need to understand a little bit about Microsoft .NET Framework. Pronounced, "dot net framework," it was designed to solve some specific challenges that were, interestingly enough, not unlike the challenges PowerShell itself was created to solve.

I've discussed a bit about how various pieces of software can expose interfaces, through which other pieces of software can tell them what to do. For example, a component that allows the user to choose a font face might expose an interface that permits larger applications like word processors or web design tools to summon the component. That kind of component-based architecture can save developers a ton of time and effort: instead of every application having to create its own font-choosing window, each application can simply tap into the same one. Windows provides tons of these common components, including ones that facilitate access to files and folders that manage network communications and much, much more.

Prior to the mid-1990s–around the time Windows NT was introduced, actually–there were few standards that described how to build these kinds of reusable, modular components. Most software programmers used the C++ programming language, and had to either build everything they needed or buy pre-made bits from someone else and incorporate those bits into their applications. The result was applications that all looked different, behaved differently, and were a pain in the butt to code.

In the mid-1990s, Microsoft introduced their Component Object Model, or COM. It was essentially a set of rules for how to build inter-application interfaces, along with a set of templates that made it easier for developers to build compliant software. Windows itself provided a huge assortment of COM-compliant components that made all the various Windows-based applications–even those from different vendors–share a common look and feel for many frequently-performed tasks. Developers could work more quickly, relying on pre-made components rather than building everything from scratch. Microsoft was by no means alone in this approach: competing technologies like JavaBeans and CORBA sought to accomplish similar outcomes, and each approach had its pros and cons.

Over time, COM's limitations became apparent. Initially, it could only work for components that all ran on the same computer—understandable, since networks were relatively rare at the time. Distributed COM, or DCOM, addressed that, enabling developers to talk to components located on entirely different computers. An application running on your desktop could talk to a DCOM component running on a server to provide you with a directory of company employees, all in a standardized, easy-to-use way. Other improvements led to COM+, which included a number of advanced features.

The evolutionary steps that COM took over time eventually got ugly, though. Certain functions were cumbersome, and the things developers needed to do started to exceed what COM could handle. As COM got bigger and bigger and changed over time, it became obvious that someone needed to sit down, re-think things, and start from scratch. All the thousands of components that had been written were still finding ways to be inconsistent in a lot of ways, which made developers' jobs harder. The limitations of DCOM's relatively proprietary communications protocols were becoming problematic as networks matured and grew larger. Security concerns that hadn't existed in 1995 started to become real threats. In the end, Microsoft committed to starting fresh.

The result, released in the early 2000s, was .NET Framework. It sought to provide a more secure, easier-to-work-with set of interfaces. In some cases, .NET simply wrapped around existing COM interfaces, making them more consistent and doing some of the heavy lifting in terms of programming so that developers could be more productive. In other cases, .NET broke new ground, creating functionality that hadn't existed previously. .NET provided the ability to have more secure, more constrained applications that could be managed more effectively in larger enterprises. .NET also sought to enable cross-platform applications, promising that developers could "code once, and run anywhere," even on non-Windows operating systems like Linux (a promise that took almost a decade to deliver on, but all good things come to those who wait). .NET provided developers with easy access to leading-edge databases, modern user interfaces, robust communications systems, and much more.

The way .NET enabled all that was via a clever set of abstractions, not wholly different from some of the abstractions in Sun Microsystems' Java language (now owned by Oracle; .NET began, in some ways, after a series of legal disputes between Microsoft and Sun over Microsoft's use of Java). .NET programmers write in one of many languages, including C#, VB.NET, and so on. Normally, a programmer writes in their language and then compiles their program into native code that can be directly run by the operating system and microprocessor of a computer. A programmer who wants their program to run on different microprocessors must recompile their code for each. .NET, however, compiled to MSIL, the Microsoft Intermediate Language, which had no tie to any given microprocessor type. When you ran the program, .NET's Common Language Runtime, or CLR, would load the MSIL and Just-in-Time, or JIT, compile it into native code for whatever machine it was running on. So you needed a CLR specific to each processor type in the world, but that was it: once the CLR could run on a machine, any .NET program could run on that machine.

.NET Framework was a huge hit. Developers could code in a variety of languages and take advantage of essentially the same features and capabilities. Applications could run across almost any recent version of Windows, ensuring wide compatibility. .NET and its main competitor, Java, became mainstays of corporate software development, providing the foundations for tens of thousands of applications.

Windows PowerShell had been written entirely in .NET. There was really no question about using it. Snover's original prototype was in .NET, and the shell was benefitting massively from much of the free functionality built into the Framework: serialization, objects, reflection, regular expressions, and a ton more. Plus, Bill Gates was running around the company pushing everyone to use .NET for their projects.

So PowerShell was written in .NET.

That would become a problem.

Windows

The 2000s had not been kind to Microsoft, or to Windows, in a number of ways. Massive security problems led to Bill Gates' 2002 "Trustworthy Computing" initiative, which promised to put security front-and-center for all Microsoft products going forward. Microsoft was still laboring under a US Department of Justice consent decree for alleged monopolistic practices involving their Internet Explorer web browser. And Windows itself was struggling to shake the perception that it was an unstable, not-ready-for-prime-time operating system. This is the world that Monad lived in, and the world in which Monad attempted to become an in-the-box Windows component.

"In-the-box," or "on-the-disc," are outdated phrases in today's world, where Windows is largely delivered over an Internet connection or pre-installed on a computer. In short, the phrase refers to components that come with the basic Windows install, as opposed to components that a user needed to go out and obtain separately. For product teams inside Microsoft, being "in-the-box" was both a blessing and a curse.

A blessing because your software would instantly be available on the millions of computers running Windows, all but guaranteeing adoption by users. Your components' bug fixes and updates could go down in the normal Windows service pack and patch system, saving your team the time and expense of developing your own servicing mechanism. All in all, a lot of benefits.

A curse, because getting "into the box" was *hard.*

Windows' engineers and architects were on a mission to make Windows *better.* They were compelled to comply with the consent decree. They were deeply concerned about security.

They didn't care for .NET.

Not that .NET wasn't stable or secure, or that it was illegal in some fashion. It's just that .NET was only in its first or second version around the mid-2000s, when Windows Longhorn's–what would eventually become Windows 2008 Server and Windows Vista, but only after five years and a major mid-development reset–and Windows' architects didn't feel .NET was fully baked.

One problem that the Windows architects objected to was .NET Framework's treatment of versioning. .NET is a large, interlinked library of software components. Say you wrote PowerShell against version 2 of the Framework. How would PowerShell behave when version 3 came out? Would users have to maintain every possible version of .NET on their systems just to ensure components would run? The short answer at the time was "yes," which was seen as absolutely acceptable for applications developed by third parties. If you bought or created an application that needed .NET Framework 2.0, then you could just install that version of the Framework right along with your application. Different versions of .NET were perfectly happy to live side-by-side for exactly that reason.

But that logic didn't fly for an operating system component. Several teams were trying to solve the "versioning problem," as it was known, which just highlighted to the Windows architects that *nobody had thought this out*. They were deeply reluctant to include any managed code components into Windows
(managed code being .NET Framework code, as opposed to the native, unmanaged code that the operating system was comprised of). Would this CLR-based .NET stuff create more bug reports? Would it make the operating system slower? Would it make Windows look bad?

They'd decided that it well might. Windows' senior leadership consisted of Microsoft's old guard. They'd been tasked with making Windows stable, predictable, and secure, and they weren't taking any chances.

Another problem was Internet Explorer, or IE. One of IE's key features was the ability to download add-ins, which would be written by third parties and used to extend the browser's functionality. Extensions and add-ins remain a key part of most modern web browsers, but they've learned a lot from IE about the security ramifications of downloading random third-party code from the Internet. In the early 2000s, IE's ActiveX snap-ins were becoming a vexing and recurring security problem, and IE was making Windows look bad. So the architects in charge of Windows itself had vowed that nothing would ship in-the-box that permitted the downloading of third-party code. This was a *bit* of a problem for PowerShell, because its entire design revolved around shipping a central engine with Windows and then permitting users to, well, download third-party code from the Internet.

Perhaps one of the best illustrations of the Windows architects' barely-concealed hatred for PowerShell is the story of how PowerShell uses live and dead objects.

This is a pretty important concept, but it's also fairly abstract. Let's quickly revisit the concept of objects. In computing, an "object" is a software representation of something. Basically, it's a data structure of sorts. An airplane object, for example, might have "properties" that describe the airplane: manufacturer, model, number of engines, number of passengers, and so on. It might also contain "methods" that represent the actions the airplane can perform: banking left or right, landing, taking off, etc.

In computing terms, a "live" object is a data structure that is still connected to whatever it represents. If you had a live airplane object, for example, you could execute its takeoff method to have the airplane physically take off in the real world. If you have a live file object representing a file on a computer's storage system, then you could rename the file, delete the file, and perform other actions.

A "dead" object, by contrast, is a static *copy* of an object's representation. For example, if you had a dead airplane object, you might be able to review its properties to see what its altitude was *when the object was created*, but that altitude property wouldn't update as it might in a live object. You couldn't call the takeoff method of a dead object, because the dead object isn't connected to the actual airplane anymore.

All of this became a thing in PowerShell.

Normally, PowerShell commands tend to return live objects. If you query a file, for example, you get an object that represents that file and is linked to it. You can use the object not only to review properties of the file, such as its name or size, but also to *change* aspects of the file, such as renaming it, deleting it, or even changing its contents. However, when you use PowerShell to connect to a remote computer and run a command, the objects you get back are dead objects. They're a static representation, and they're no longer linked to the remote computer. Making them live objects isn't practical, and would consume a great deal of computing and network resources.

Snover says, "If you take a look at the core design decisions throughout PowerShell, you'll see a common thread: I don't trust networks. Networks fail. Networks fail all the freaking time. They fail in binary ways and they sorta fail and sometimes they just get slow and wonky. I don't trust networks."

WMI used live objects across a Distributed Component Object Model (DCOM) connection. "If you get a local or a remote WMI object, they behave the same way," Snover explains. "Access a method and WMI turns it into a network call," so that the method can execute on the computer that the object came from. "The problem then is that EVERY SINGLE TIME YOU CALL A METHOD, IT CAN FAIL," because of the vagaries of networks. "That is why you get dead objects in PowerShell...you either get the object or you don't, but if you get it, then you can deal with it with safety and surety. The success of working with that object no longer depends upon the network."

"So then WHY ever have live objects? This was how we were going to be able to be light enough to run GUIs on PowerShell. Remember, the goal was to write all the GUIs with PowerShell underneath. The only way that would work is if PS had live objects." Those live objects are always local, though, and so they don't depend on the network.

The Windows Architecture team thought that this inconsistency was a "gotcha" they could use to defeat PowerShell during a Bill Gates review session. "BillG reviews," as many Microsoft people at the time called them, were famously intense. Bill would get very passionate about software, and he'd let you know if he thought you weren't doing the right thing. There'd be cursing, name-calling, yelling, and lots more. So the Windows Architecture folks seeded the idea that PowerShell was inconsistent, because *sometimes* it returned live objects, but other times it returned dead objects. Consistency should be key, they suggested.

Jeffrey Snover walked into this BillG review and could tell Bill was already pretty convinced of the Architecture guys' arguments. But then it was his turn to talk.

"Inconsistency is great!" he said. He knew that he needed to break the conversational thread, and saying something crazy would do it. It caught Bill's attention, for sure.

Snover removed his new bifocal eyeglasses, and pointed at the thin line that bisected each lens. "These are new, and the lens is inconsistent," Snover explains. "The top half is optimized for seeing remote things, and the bottom half is optimized for seeing local things." Prior to getting these, he said, he'd had two separate pairs of glasses, each perfectly consistent and good for only one thing. He spent all day swapping glasses back and forth. When he got the new ones, the inconsistency was literally right there in front of his eyes, all the time. That lasted for about two hours, though, and he barely noticed it after that. Instead, he was just more efficient, because he had one tool that could work well in two different situations. The inconsistency of the lenses provided a more consistent view of the world.

Snover won the argument.

He says, "It is worth noting that from the very beginning, BillG 'got' PowerShell and loved it. The first time I showed it to him, he said, 'this is clearly an example of going from the worst in the industry (Cmd.exe) to the best in the industry.' The problem was all the people between Bill and us. The reality is that having Bill on your side didn't really matter that much."

He adds, "Interesting note: the same WinArch architect that was adamant that all the GUIs had to be layered over PowerShell (and therefore we HAD to have Live Objects) was also the one leading the charge to kill PowerShell in the BillG review because we had both live and dead objects. I think that guy was so blinded by his desire to f-ing kill off PowerShell that he didn't mind his own inconsistency."

The running joke on the Monad team at the time was that the Windows Architecture team had established seven "gates," or requirements, that they needed to pass in order to be included in-the-box. Once the team had passed all of those, they discovered the eighth gate, which was simple, "hell, no."

Jim Truher labeled this "StinkyKick" cartoon by Andy Helms to reflect how the Monad team felt at the time.

Charlie Chase, a GPM inside Microsoft at the time, remembers filing the Design Change Request, or DCR, asking for PowerShell to be included in-the-box.

Brian Valentine, the man in charge of Windows Client at the time, denied it. Specifically, he told Chase to withdraw the DCR. Chase refused, telling Valentine that he'd need to deny the DCR on the record. Which Valentine did.

PowerShell was without a home.

Or was it? After all, Windows wasn't Microsoft's only strategic product.

Exchange

One of Microsoft's other strategic products–and in 2006 arguably one of its *most* strategic products–was Microsoft Exchange Server. In today's cloud-based world, where Microsoft Office 365 runs many companies' email with no need for an onsite server, it's hard to imagine that, in 2006, most large companies ran *dozens* of Exchange Server computers. Sure, Exchange Server required the Windows operating system, but *Exchange* is what you were buying.

And the Exchange team had an automation problem.

Remember, back in 2000 Microsoft had acquired Hotmail, and Windows' lack of administrative automation capabilities was highlighted as a key challenge to migrating Hotmail to Windows. In fact, Hotmail was migrated to *Windows,* not *Exchange.* The Exchange team was aware that administrative automation was a problem, and with Exchange 12–which would become known as Exchange Server 2007–they were prepared to do something about it.

But these things take time. Figure that Exchange Server 2007 probably started development just before the release of its predecessor, Exchange Server 2003. These four- to five-year product cycles were the norm inside Microsoft at the time, so when planning for Exchange Server 2007 kicked off, the need to improve administrative automation was very much on everyone's mind. And that timeframe closely coincided with the development of Windows Longhorn, where PowerShell had just been denied entry.

Now, the Exchange team was not only well aware of their automation problem, they were completely on top of it. They'd designed their own automation solution–essentially, an Application Programming Interface, or API–to solve the problem.

At the time, Dave Thompson had moved from Windows to work on Exchange Server. Snover and Thompson had a long-standing relationship: when Snover took the job at Microsoft, he'd intended to work under Thompson. "I never joined Microsoft, I joined Dave Thompson," Snover recalls. In fact, right after Snover had faxed in his letter of acceptance for the position, Thompson called and said, "Guess what! You're not going to be working for me after all! We had a re-org!" When Snover eventually took over the Kermit team and made it the PowerShell team, he was under Thompson for a while before Dave left for Exchange.

But relationships are important at any company. One afternoon, Snover ran across Thompson in a hallway and started explaining what the PowerShell team was working on. Thompson said, "Hey, you should talk to my Exchange guys–they're working on this and might want to hear what you're up to. Maybe they should be using this Monad thing."

The Exchange team wasn't really interested in Snover's new shell; they figured they had their situation under control, and they didn't need an outsider complicating things. But Snover needed a product to ship with, so he and the team dug in their heels and set out to become the best solution Exchange could have.

When the Exchange team said, "Well, your shell would have to do A, B, and C in order for us to consider it," the PowerShell team made A, B, and C happen. When the Exchange team came back asking for X, Y, and Z, they got those too. The Exchange team was a tough customer, but when they realized that the PowerShell team was essentially catering to them–and doing a great job of it–they relented.

So the PowerShell team changed their strategy: PowerShell 1.0 would be primarily lined up to support Exchange Server, not Windows. And the Exchange Server team was betting *big*.

Part of the sales pitch for PowerShell had always been its ability to write a small amount of code and get maximum reuse from it. By writing a PowerShell cmdlet (pronounced "command-let") to, say, add a new email mailbox for a user, you would be instantly solving several problems. That cmdlet could be run from the command-line by an administrator who was comfortable doing so. It could be added to a script to help automate a larger business process. And it could hide behind the scenes of a graphical user interface, or GUI, for administrators who were more comfortable clicking icons and buttons than they were typing commands. The Exchange Server team bought the sales pitch and decided to build their *entire administrative interface* atop PowerShell. Exchange Server would depend utterly on PowerShell for administration: PowerShell 1.0 would ship with Exchange Server, and it would drive the entire administrative experience.

It was a *big* bet.

You're talking about a team that *already had a fully functional GUI* basically tossing that out and writing *brand-new code* in .NET to manage an entire, incredibly complex product, and then building a new GUI on top of that–a process that was at least simplified since the underlying code was done. It was a huge investment, and a lot of work.

And with Exchange Server looking like the best way to get Power-Shell out the door–"I remember," Charlie Chase said, "convincing Jeffrey Snover that 'shipping is a feature'"–the PowerShell team committed themselves to making sure Exchange Server would succeed. Numerous evolutions to PowerShell itself, as well as what the team prioritized, focused on making PowerShell *work* for the Exchange automation effort.

As an aside, the Exchange team was probably more forward-looking in many ways than the PowerShell team itself. Remoting, for example, was an Exchange team demand that didn't *quite* make it into v1 but that did ship in v2 to support Exchange's new cloud-based use cases. Exchange developed a just-in-time, minimal authority model of permissions that, years later, became the basis for PowerShell's Just Enough Administration, or JEA, toolkit. Exchange drove much of PowerShell's progress not only through the v1 ship, but also well into the shell's future.

And PowerShell supported Exchange well into the future, too: one of Exchange's leaders later said, "PowerShell was *the* technology that allowed Microsoft to go to the cloud." Exchange was Microsoft's first cloud product, in the form of outsourced, cloud-based email in Office 365, and "we never could have deployed or scaled without PowerShell. We never could have gotten on DevOps and iterated–it never would have worked."

It was a bet, and an investment, that paid off: Exchange Server 2007 shipped with PowerShell v1 built right in (although PowerShell was also available as a standalone, download-it-yourself component).

Arguably the biggest Microsoft server product aside from Windows Server itself, Exchange put PowerShell into the hands of tens of thousands of administrators. Thanks to the GUI-atop-PowerShell architecture, many of those admins didn't even know PowerShell was lurking under the hood. But, for the more experienced crowd that needed automation to manage large environments, Exchange Server 2007 was a paradigm shift.

Now if the team could *just* get PowerShell into Windows.

Windows, Again

With PowerShell's triumphant 2006 release as part of Exchange Server 2007–although you could also download the shell all by itself from Microsoft's website–it was time to try and get back "in the box" with Windows itself. The motto for v2 of PowerShell was "PowerShell everywhere," meaning the team wanted PowerShell to ship with Windows, putting the shell everywhere Windows was.

The team worked incredibly hard to clear all of the Windows

Architecture team's gates to inclusion in Windows. They went through BillG reviews, they ticked off all the checkboxes they were given, and finally had to deal with management and *politics.*

Brian Valentine had been the primary high-level objector to PowerShell's inclusion in Windows, and he was the one who'd denied the Design Change Request (DCR) files by Charlie Chase to let PowerShell in.

Bob Muglia, higher in the org chart than Valentine, set up a private meeting between the two men. Snover has a colorful, amusing, and incredibly NSFW turn of phrase for that conversation, and if you're ever at a cocktail party with him, ask him about it. By the way, he drinks Budweiser. Not Bud Light.

After the meeting, Muglia sent out the kind of email you'd expect a high-level, professional, corporate executive to send out: "I appreciate your perspective, I understand your concerns, but this is the business decision and we're going to move ahead." It's the type of email you send out to try and allow all sides to save face even though, in some decisions, not everyone can have their way all at the same time. If you've been advocating for something other than what becomes the final decision, it's an honorable way out of the argument.

Valentine didn't take it.

He hit "reply all" to a list that's been described as "pretty much everyone," and launched an impassioned, emotional diatribe against PowerShell being included in Windows. This was likely driven at least somewhat by him supporting his team members who were themselves fighting to keep PowerShell out of Windows, but it was too late. The decision had been made, and the next version of Windows would ship with Windows PowerShell v2 in the box.

PowerShell was now real. It wasn't just an Exchange thing, and it was about to be in the hands of every Windows user on Earth.

v2

In addition to being the first version of Windows PowerShell to ship *with* Windows (the team's motto for v2 was "PowerShell Everywhere," and shipping in the box was how they planned to achieve that), the story of v2 is worth telling.

Kenneth Hansen was a Principal Program Manager at Microsoft, and he'd joined the Monad team early on, taking responsibility for the main API, Extensible Type System (ETS), programmer experience, and more. By v2, he'd become the Principal Program Manager in charge of the entire team.

Hemant Mahawar (who signed his emails "He-Man™") joined the team as a Program Manager just as v1 was readying for release. For v2, he handled the session state and session configuration technologies, and took over Remoting when the PM in charge of that feature left the team.

> If you're not familiar with Microsoft product teams, they're roughly split into two main components: Program Management and Software Development (or Software Engineering). Program Managers, or PMs, do most of the designing and high-level project management-type tasks; Software Engineers actually write the code. There are hierarchies within both sides, meaning you'll have Lead Developers, various ranks of Program Managers, and so on. Architects, like Jeffrey Snover, sit above and apart from them all, working directly with Program Managers on functional specifications and often consulting with Engineering on critical implementation details. That's all a bit oversimplified, but it helps to understand how different people collaborate as a product comes to life.

Hansen remembers v2 being a whirlwind. The team spent just three weeks planning it and about eighteen months creating it. V2 was meant to be "a better v1," meaning the team wanted to invest in what was already working well and make it work even *better,* as well as bring some shiny and important new features into the product. Remoting was the first, as it had *nearly* been ready to ship in v1 and was essential to the Exchange Server team's plans to enable a scalable, cloud-based version of Exchange.

Hansen remembers one of the first design meetings. "I've got this spreadsheet, and I'm collecting everyone's ideas. I'm kind of sorting and organizing everything. We've got eight key people in the room–Snover, Bruce Payette, me, and so on." They needed to quickly stack-rank everyone's ideas so that they could have a sense of priorities and what they would or wouldn't be able to accomplish in the tight timeframe they had. Kenneth proposed a process for accomplishing that ranking, and it was something he felt would be simple and efficient. One person in the room, however, didn't like that process and wanted to do something more complex and time-consuming that, the argument went, would be fairer and more accurate in the end. Snover was kind of fighting Hansen's process as well, and everyone in the room was getting frustrated. They'd spent the first quarter of their meeting time just arguing about the process when Hansen finally said, "Look, we're doing it my way for the next 45 minutes, and if it doesn't work, we'll try something else the next time." Everyone agreed, the meeting moved on, and Hansen's process actually wound up working great.

Afterwards, still annoyed with how obstinate Snover had seemed to be about it all, Hansen pulled him aside and asked what the problem was. "Oh, I just didn't see it," Snover replied. "But it was good, it worked fine." Snover simply hadn't understood until he saw the process in action, and then he was fine with it. Hansen says his biggest takeaway from that incident was to always assume good intent. "Even really brilliant people can sometimes genuinely 'not get it,' but it's not malicious." Hansen says you also need to be aware that not everyone speaks the same "language;" something that can be crystal clear to you can be muddled or confusing to someone else—no matter how smart you both are.

Mahawar remembers the "R.I.P. Board," where the team would write down features and ideas that they hadn't had time to get to, in hopes that they'd be able to circle back one day and do them all.

The v2 time was all about moving quickly, but moving with agreement and alignment. The team didn't have the time to design an entire API and *then* discuss it, because that would take two weeks that they simply didn't have. So they adopted a five-slide pitch approach: if you wanted something in v2, you had to pitch it in five slides. What are you proposing? What problem does it solve? Who's the audience? What's the user experience? It allowed everyone to quickly come to alignment on the proposal and to move forward. Today, software designers often focus on something called "Human-Centered Design," which puts the software's users, and their needs and assumptions, at the center of every design. The concept wasn't widespread in 2007 when PowerShell v2 was being designed, but the five-slide pitch was firmly about creating a product that, at its center, featured human beings writing code to get a specific kind of job done.

PowerShell v2 is perhaps best known for three headline features: remoting, modules, and its Integrated Scripting Environment, or ISE. Remoting, as has been mentioned elsewhere in this book, was very nearly a v1 feature, but the team couldn't get it fully stable in time for the v1 deadline. It therefore became an obvious v2 feature, requiring a minimal amount of incremental investment to complete. Remoting is an excellent illustration of how much careful thought went into v1, because once it was finally released in v2 remoting went through almost no functional or design changes for several years.

Mahawar remembers remoting being more of a political challenge. The Exchange Server team–who'd been treated as first-class citizens for the v1 release–had some pretty strong demands for the new remoting feature. As Microsoft transitioned more and more customers to Exchange Online (which became part of Office 365), the Exchange team wanted administrators to be able to remote in to their Exchange Online service, and to be able to manage it just as quickly as if it was installed on-premises. That's impossible, of course: anything traversing a network is going to be slower than if it was local, and the PowerShell team pointed that out. "Fine," the Exchange team countered. "We'll accept 1.1x speeds, but no more." Snover and Hansen spent considerable time managing the relationship, and reminding the Exchange folks about the simple physics of networking: you can't always control network latency when you're talking about a global audience, for example. Exchange also pushed hard for a specific Role-Based Access Control, or RBAC, model. "Tell us the requirements," the PowerShell team would say, "and we'll develop the model." Snover knew that Exchange needed to be successful, but that *other* teams would also need to be successful. He and the rest of the PowerShell team wanted to serve that greater good.

After v2's three-week planning stage was complete, Hansen did a five-slide pitch for modules and got the high-level design out of the way quickly. Modules, at a basic level, needed to be a better way of packaging commands into manageable units, because the team was looking to add *hundreds* of commands in v2. Bruce Payette understood the need right away, and he and Ken kind of conspired to make modules succeed. But Hansen was, at the time, being pulled in every direction, and so another program manager on the team took ownership of modules. They wound up writing a *very* detailed specification–"maybe a little too detailed," Hansen recalls–some of which was way too complex and would likely not work out. Payette was asked to collaborate because at the time he likely knew more than anyone on the team about how PowerShell worked as a complete system. The PM would bring the spec to Payette, and Payette would beat it up. Bruce had a clear personal vision for how modules would work, but the PM also had a clear vision– and some compelling arguments against some of what Payette felt was right. That kind of intra-team tension is not only common in software development, it's often seen as healthy and desirable: get all the right minds on the problem, let them fight it out, and you'll probably wind up with the best possible product in the end. But it was time-consuming, and it meant that modules were running late with respect to the overall v2 timeline.

Too late, in fact. Remember, the primary goal of v2 was to ship in Windows, and Windows had a fairly far-out code lockdown milestone, where everything needed to either be done and working or be cut from the product. Snover, Hansen, and others on the team petitioned their Windows overlords for patience as they triaged modules. Unfortunately, they were nowhere near ready, with some serious complexities holding things up. "We can't ship it like this," Hansen remembers thinking. "We either have to cut them or redo them."

Fortunately, the PowerShell team had a lot of scrappy, dedicated individuals working on it, and they all pitched in. Payette, Program Manager Dan Harman, and others rolled up their sleeves and promised to get it done. What they turned out was simpler and far more usable, and wound up shipping in v2. It was an interesting time, as some of them remember, because v2 was otherwise stable and working, but one element–a key element, no less–was being redone from scratch at very close to the last possible minute.

Like modules, the Integrated Scripting Environment, or ISE, wasn't in the original plan for v2. Program Manager Refaat Issa (who commonly signed his emails "Ref@") had pushed hard for it. At the time, the only built-in tool for writing PowerShell scripts was Windows Notepad, a bare-bones text editor that offered zero assistance to a script author. "Real" programmers were accustomed to Integrated Development Environments, or IDEs, like Microsoft Visual Studio. IDEs provided numerous tools, cues, helpers, and so on to make coding more efficient and less error-prone, and Issa strongly felt that PowerShell needed something similar if it was going to engage and grow an audience. Hansen couldn't sign off on it, though, because the team was already well into coding v2 and was fully committed.

"What if I do it?" Issa asked. Microsoft Program Managers aren't formally expected to be software programmers, but many are, and Issa was one of those. "Tell you what," Hansen said, "you get a week, and if you come back with a plan that costs me nothing, then I'll look at it." So Issa did. He worked with Microsoft's Visual Studio team, getting permission to use some of their editor's code, which would significantly bootstrap the ISE's development. PowerShell itself helped out a lot, since many of its native features eased the task of writing a decent code editor. The ISE wound up requiring about half of Issa's time along with half of a software engineer's time, and it got done.

> The ISE also solved another problem for the team, which was Unicode character sets. The ancient Command Host that PowerShell used–the same one used by the MS-DOS-like Cmd.exe Windows shell–couldn't display Unicode character sets, meaning many potential users couldn't use PowerShell in their native language. The ISE, using more modern components, was fully Unicode-capable, opening PowerShell up to a wider global audience.

The ISE wound up getting a major overhaul for v3 after the team saw how much it was enabling their audience, but it never would have happened if Issa hadn't volunteered to take on the original ISE as, essentially, a side project. Side efforts were a big thing in Microsoft at the time, and you'd be surprised at how many headline product features started that way. That approach went away for a while as Microsoft slowly moved into Agile development approaches, but now, as Microsoft commits more toward open-source software and more community engagement, you see side projects contributing to more and more products again.

PowerShell v2 also made a contribution of sorts to Windows itself. The team needed to figure out a way to distribute patches for PowerShell, should the need arise. For Windows Server 2003 and Windows XP, it was easy: bundle everything into an executable (EXE) or Windows Installer (MSI) file. But Windows Vista, where PowerShell v2 would be shipping, had introduced a new servicing mechanism in the form of Microsoft Update, or MSU, files. Much of the structure and functionality of today's MSUs, which are still in use as a servicing system, came from PowerShell. As the first shipping-with-Windows application written in .NET Framework managed code, PowerShell had specific versioning and dependency requirements that MSUs needed to support.

DESIGN

Design Decisions and Coding Stories

From its earliest days, PowerShell's designers wanted to stress *consistency*. For example, PowerShell commands all start with a verb: Get, Set, Remove, Start, Stop, and so on. This verbs should be drawn from a limited set of a few dozen "approved" verbs. Doing so helps *protect learning*, because once you learn what a "Get"

command does, you can automatically start to infer things about *every other command* that uses that same verb. Your investment in learning is *protected*, because whatever you've learned will be used consistently throughout the shell. It's probably one of the first instances of shell design where the designers acknowledged the investment they would be asking of their users, and so they made a promise to maximize the return on that investment. It's a hugely valuable lesson that GUI designers learned from the outset, but that computer language designers rarely seem to fully embrace.

Decision-Making Principles

In its earliest days, the PowerShell team put together a list of principles, almost like values, that would guide its decisions. These were stack-ranked, and when a conflict arose, the team would look and see which principles were affected. The higher-ranked principle would "win" the conflict.

Snover gives an example of this approach, which serves as a cautionary tale for getting that stack-ranking right. IBM's Micro-Channel Architecture, or MCA bus, was created in 1987 as an advance over the older Industry Standard Architecture (ISA) bus that preceded it. In designing the new bus, IBM's architects also created a stack-ranked list of principles, such as "speed," "signal reliability," "backward compatibility," "ease of manufacturing," and so on. Unfortunately, "backward compatibility" was very low in the stack-rank, so as the team had to make decisions about which way to go, they moved further and further away from compatibility with the older PCI bus. As a result, the MCA bus was a technical marvel—fast, reliable, easy to build, and so on—but it was utterly incompatible with anything that had come before, and it wound up being used in only one series of IBM computers before it was abandoned.

The PowerShell team spent a *lot* of time developing its principles, some of which you'll read about elsewhere in this book, like, "protecting the learning investment." Snover and other team members credit that list of principles with not only helping them make the right decisions for PowerShell's long-term success, but for enabling different bits of the team to move faster and more independently when needed. Some of those principles (not necessarily in their final order) include:

- Security
- Supportability
- Consistency
- Performance
- Scale-up
- Scale-down
- Discoverability
- Extensibility
- Reliability

Program Manager Kenneth Hansen remembers a higher-level set of principles that, he says, a lot of people don't fully remember. These weren't designed as much to help resolve conflicts in the decision-making process, but more as high-level mission statements for what PowerShell needed to become. "We did PowerShell because nothing else would work," Hansen remembers. "We ended up with PowerShell because we weren't a text-based operating system. We were everything—files, .NET, COM, WMI, everything—and that forced us into doing PowerShell. Jeffrey then had the vision of the pipeline, and those led us to create a language that wasn't a clean language. And it wasn't intended to be clean! It's meant to get the job done, and to some extent, that was the overriding principle: I can do my job."

Hansen's first principle is what he calls the **Principle of And**. "We're going to be a shell. *And* a scripting language. *And* a systems language. We're going to do .NET, *and* COM, *and* ADO, *and* CSV, *and* WMI. You name it, it all goes through the same substrate. We're doing to do command-line *and* GUI." Those are unusual decisions in software design, where designers typically try to scope the software down to a well-defined, manageable set of tasks.

Next is the **Principle of 2AM**, meaning, "it just has to work." It's 2am, you're trying to get your job done, and you have to be able to push the Return button on the keyboard knowing that your job is on the line. Features like the common -Confirm and -WhatIf parameters, which enable an administrator to take "baby steps" and verify what they're about to do, came from this principle.

Hansen offers a possibly-not-politically-correct analogy: in past military engagements, US soldiers were issued expensive M-16 rifles. In many instances though, soldiers in the field would discard their US-issued weapons and instead opt for cheaply and less well-made alternatives like the AK-47. The AK-47 is a fairly poorly made rifle: it's not necessarily all that precise, but when you're crawling through mud and water and dirt and grit, the AK-47 has "just enough slop" to continue working through that abuse. By contrast, and M-16 is a more precision-engineered device that will jam easily. PowerShell, Hansen says, was meant to be more like an AK-47, with plenty of "slop" for administrators. For example, many commands are capable of performing somewhat dangerous tasks. While PowerShell might warn you that you're about to do something wrong, you'll nearly always find a -Force parameter that will let you do it anyway. "Having principles like this affects every-thing, and becomes very thoughtful," Hansen says. Jeffrey Snover would later amend this analogy, and state that "programming with PowerShell is like programming with hand grenades." PowerShell wasn't designed as a tight, strict language the way that many programming languages are. Instead, it allows for "slop." There are many ways to get things done, and the "right" way is the way that's quickest for you, personally, in your moment of need.

His third principle is the **Principle of Leverage**, which reflects the team's commitment to "preserving your learning investment."

If you learn something, PowerShell makes that investment worth your while, because you'll get to use that same knowledge over and over. When PowerShell v2 introduced Advanced Functions—originally known as "script cmdlets"—they leveraged the same structure and form as "real" cmdlets, helping leverage what cmdlet authors already knew, and leveraging much of the same code within the shell itself. The concept of PowerShell's common parameters, which apply to every cmdlet in the shell, comes from this same principle.

Usability Testing

Kenneth Hansen believes that PowerShell may have been the first software product where the core Application Programming Interface, or API, was usability tested.

Usability testing is common in the software industry, although it usually applies to graphical interfaces. For example, if you're designing a new word processor, you might get it to the point where a user could begin working with it. You'd then sit a few dozen users down with the product and ask them to accomplish a particular set of tasks. You'd then record them, and watch how they tried to perform the task. Ideally, you've designed a product that's intuitive, so users don't need a lot of instruction and can just "figure it out." But if you see them fumbling, you look carefully at where they're stuck, and you see if you can engineer a better, more *usable* product in your next iteration. Microsoft is deeply committed to this kind of usability testing: the company has entire lab spaces dedicated to that kind of work.

But, as far as Hansen knows, nobody had ever done the same thing with an API.

PowerShell's success, the team knew, would hinge largely on developers being able to create cmdlets that ran in PowerShell.

Without cmdlets, PowerShell is essentially useless. The shell is an engine, and cmdlets actually accomplish the tasks administrators need to perform. Therefore, the ability for developers to quickly and efficiently create cmdlets was critical.

So the team sat some developers down, showed them the cmdlet API and frameworks they'd created, and asked the developers to write cmdlets. They watched them, much as you would in a GUI-based usability test, to see where they succeeded and where they stumbled. "Most teams, when they build an API, they talk to people," Hansen says, "and they get feedback. But they don't actually do usability testing." The team's original objective, he remembers, was to ensure even a Visual Basic .NET developer could successfully produce cmdlets. VB developers in a typical business were often less experienced, and often lacked formal software development education, but they represented a large potential audience that the team wanted to address. Through successive rounds of usability testing, the team made numerous changes to their framework and API, making it progressively easier and more consistent for developers to work with. Even tasks like specifying cmdlet metadata was made easier through that process. Those same structures were then applied to Advanced Functions in PowerShell v2, enabling them to benefit from all that prior work.

Being Verbose

PowerShell was also a marked departure from what had become an unwritten commandment in computer software design. Bill Gates had, in the distant past, rewritten the prompt in his BASIC language from "Ready" to "Ok," because the latter saved three bytes of memory. The PowerShell team acknowledged that memory and disk space were no longer urgent constraints for most people, and so minimizing their use would be a far lower priority than minimizing users' *time*. If there was a usage pattern that was quick and easy to understand, they'd implement that pattern, even if it wasn't disk- or memory-efficient. To this day, PowerShell scripts are rarely the fastest-running kind of code, but they're amongst the easiest to write. For example, this is a pretty memory-heavy operation, if run in a folder that contains a lot of files:

```
Get-ChildItem | Select Name
```

Every file and folder has to be retrieved and run through the pipeline just to get all of their names. Basically, you're getting *way* more data—including file sizes, last modified dates, and more— than you need, and then filtering it down to just what you wanted. Any database administrator would cringe at that pattern, because it's wasteful in terms of processing time and memory. PowerShell *enables* that model though, because it's straightforward and easy to learn. It "spends" computing resources to "gain" ease of use.

Providers

Kenneth Hansen was the Program Manager originally in charge of the Providers, or PSProviders, aspect of PowerShell. Providers were meant to provide an easy way for administrators to approach a wide variety of radically different systems, particularly around data storage. They used a single set of commands for manipulation and management, with the Provider itself "adapting" the underlying system so that, more or less, everything looked like a file system. Administrators are already deeply familiar and comfortable with file systems, so "adapting" other things to look like a file system helps leverage what administrators have already learned.

And so *Providers* were another of PowerShell's Big Ideas. Much of computer administration involves reading and writing data from various data stores. The file system is one such data store, and on Windows there are others: the system registry, Active Directory, environment variables, and more. The team started doing the math on all the commands they'd need...

- Get-RegistryValue
- Set-RegistryValue
- Get-FileAttribute
- Set-FileAttribute
- Get-EnvironmentVariable
- Set-EnvironmentVariable

...and they realized there was going to be a lot of repeated effort. After some brainstorming, they decided instead to create a generic set of commands:

- Get-Item
- Set-Item
- Remove-Item

And so on. These would have the ability to generically deal with "any" basic data store. To bridge the gap between their generic model and a specific data store, like the registry or the file system, PowerShell would have *providers*. In many ways, PowerShell providers act as *adapters*, turning a data store-specific set of APIs into a generic set that the "Item" commands could deal with. This also helped to protect users' learning investment: you could learn a relatively small set of a dozen or so commands, and re-use those same commands, in the same patterns, across any data store for which a provider had been written. Writing a provider was a bit more complex, but it's something that a professional programmer could do *once*.

Hansen wishes they'd had more time to work on Providers, though. "The API [for creating a provider] is just too hard." Notably, the Providers API was never subjected to the rigorous usability testing that PowerShell's "main" API went through, the team's feeling at the time having been one of, "only serious developers will do this, so we don't need to worry about it being complex." But still, the team itself wound up re-writing the Registry provider *three times* before v1 released. Hansen remembers "separation characters" being a special challenge: in a normal file system, a slash (forward slashes in Unix and Linux, backward slashes in Windows) is used to separate the different components of a file's location and name: C:\Folder\File.txt indicates a file named File.txt, living in a directory named Folder on the C: drive. But the Windows Registry was never designed to be accessed via command-line, and so it didn't have a "native" separation character. Slashes—both kinds—were legal parts of *names*, and therefore couldn't reliably used to separate items. In the end, the team came up with a solution, but to this day it isn't as elegant as Hansen had hoped to achieve.

Ctrl+C

Since the earliest days, the Ctrl+C keyboard combination has been a "break" signal to the computer. Even in the mainframe days, pressing Ctrl+C would interrupt the current task and return control to the user. In a modern shell, a runaway command could "lock up" the entire shell; Ctrl+C provided a quick way to "break" out of that and regain control of the command-line.

Jim Truher doesn't remember the specifics ("a red haze descended on me surrounding this episode"), but he recalls attending a meeting where the team was going through the work items and scheduling. An engineering manager suggested that Ctrl+C not be implemented in PowerShell, because there was a workaround for it. The manager explained that "the little red 'X' in the top corner could take care of the problem," Truher says, referring to the button, present on most windows in the Windows operating system, which would close the window. That's not quite the same thing as regaining control, though.

Snover remembers Truher pointing out that, completely outside of Microsoft's control, third-party cmdlets could hang a process, and the user would need to kill that process.

"Kill it using Task Manager," the engineering manager insisted.

"But what if they have ten PowerShell sessions?" Snover and Truher protested. They would all simply show as "PowerShell.exe" in the Task Manager, so "how would they know which one to kill?"

"Go to the other nine sessions, type $PID, and don't kill any of those process IDs." The remaining one would be the "hung" one and could be killed.

"Jim's head exploded," Snover says.

"It was one of those times where I totally lost it," Truher admits. "I remember being speechless, and I don't remember if I said anything career-limiting at the time, but I definitely had career-limiting thoughts."

Truher says he came away with a couple of things. "That manager had *absolutely no idea* what we were building, and was a danger to the project (and probably society in general). Further, I had to do everything I could to protect the project from such nitwits." Also, "we had a number of people on the team [who] didn't write scripts. I was appalled and tried to marginalize the work they were doing."

"I remember that episode well," Hilal Al-Hilali agrees. "I had been told some smart people were working on PowerShell. Then Jim [Truher] comes and tells me about Ctrl+C. The conversation left me scratching my head—'smart people' wanted to cut Ctrl+C? I tried to imagine under what conditions you could cut this feature and could not come up with any."

Ctrl+C made it into PowerShell, and remains to this day.

Extensible Type System

Another Big Idea? The ability to dynamically add management-specific functionality to software that hadn't originally been build with management in mind. PowerShell's Extensible Type System, or ETS, was the answer. The underlying .NET Framework objects that PowerShell used could be extended on-the-fly with new properties, methods, and other functionality that was specific to administrative tasks. The ETS eliminated the need to re-do all the work that had already been done in .NET, and made .NET's functionality more specific to systems administrators.

For example, an administrator might want to know how long a given process had been running on a machine, but the native .NET Framework object that represents processes doesn't contain that information. So the ETS was used to add a property that retrieved that information from elsewhere, and added it to the Process objects displayed in PowerShell.

The ETS was also used to improve on the consistency of the .NET Framework. For example, PowerShell has several systems that look for a "Name" property, simply because *most* objects *do* have a "Name" property, and because when they do, it's usually pretty descriptive and useful. Process objects, however, have a "ProcessName" property, which is inconsistent. So the ETS adds a "Name" property, which is an alias to the underlying "Process-Name" property. The original object structure is still there, but it's enhanced with something that's more consistent.

How Parameters Became Cmdlets

PowerShell's original model always included the ability to filter data, sort it, produce lists and tables, and so on. In fact, the basic structure for one of the original concepts of a cmdlet looked a bit like this:

```
1   Get-File -Where Name=*.txt -Sort Name -First 10
```

There's a problem with that pattern, though: almost universally, command-line syntax permits the user to provide arguments in any order they want, without affecting the outcome of the command. Therefore, the above command should be able to be written like this as well:

```
1   Get-File -First 10 -Where Name=*.txt -Sort Name
```

Problem is, that command *wouldn't* necessarily produce the same results, would it? If you're sorting the items first, and then taking the first ten, that's a different result than if you take the first ten and *then* sort them, right? And so the cmdlets had to be broken down into smaller "monads." Modern PowerShell might look something like this instead:

```
1   Get-File |
2   Where-Object Name -like *.txt |
3   Sort-Object Name |
4   Select-Object -First 10
```

In practice, that could be written all on one line; it's broken down here to accommodate the limits of the printed page. But by taking those arguments like -Where and -Sort, and instead making them their own standalone cmdlets, administrators have the ability to specify their order of execution. Stringing them together in a pipeline produces the desired results.

Parameters: - vs. /

In his pilot and original specifications for Monad, Snover originally implemented parameters to use the forward-slash character:

```
1  Get-Service /computername WHATEVER
```

The idea was to be consistent with DCL (Digital Command Language) standard. After all, Windows had been inspired by Digital's VMS operating system, and so turning to DCL for inspiration seems sensible.

Others pushed back, pointing out that the / was inconsistent with Unix, and they were meant to be using Posix more as a model for the shell.

The team took a moment to think about who their customers really were. While the DCL connection to Windows was clear enough to them, the fact was that the world contained a few hundred VMS administrators, and tens of thousands of Unix administrators. DCL compatibility, they decided, was not worth focusing on. *That* led to a re-thinking of the core command-line syntax in PowerShell. Snover was convinced that longer, verbose parameter names—like "computername" versus something more obscure like "cn"—was critical for self-documentation and clarity. But he agreed to change from / to - as a means of identifying parameters:

```
1  Get-Service -ComputerName WHATEVER
```

Payette came back in a day or two with the new implementation. Snover says, "I was shocked and delighted by this, and after we tried it out with more customers and partners, we decided to go with it."

WHERE: The Elevation of the ScriptBlock

Anyone who's used PowerShell for even a little while knows the Where-Object command. Its purpose is to accept objects from the pipeline, examine them according to some criteria that you specify, and then only pass along objects that meet your criteria. It's a "filter" of sorts: get me all of the running processes, but only keep the ones that are using a lot of memory right now.

The original concept for the command had it using a Structured Query Language (SQL)-inspired syntax:

```
1   Get-Process |
2   Where -Expression "virtualmemorysize -gt 100000"
```

This started to create some difficulties as they dug into the implementation, though. Snover credits Bruce Payette with the solution:

```
1   Get-Process |
2   Where { $_.virtualmemorysize -gt 100000 }
```

In this variant, which is what eventually went into the product, the characters form a *script block*. It's a tiny little chunk of executable code. The $_ notation represents "whatever object was piped into the command," which in this case would be a Process object. This became an easy way to use object-style notation, such as following the object with a period and then the property you wanted to refer to. This also solidified the concept of script blocks, which wound up becoming a foundational element in PowerShell and enabling a great many other features in a consistent manner.

-WhatIf, -Confirm, and -Verbose

Snover says that one of the things he's most proud of in PowerShell is the *value for lines of code* that was created with the ShouldProcess() feature.

The idea with the -WhatIf and -Confirm parameters is that a cmdlet or function can choose to implement them. If they do, then whatever code performs the command's "main" work gets wrapped in a conditional statement:

```
If (ShouldProcess(Object, Action))
        Do Action on Object
Else
        Don't
```

If the user runs the command and specifies -WhatIf, then PowerShell displays a message about *what it would have done*, but doesn't actually take the action. If the user specifies -Confirm, then ShouldProcess() basically creates a Yes/No prompt, asking the user if they're sure, and doing so for *each* item that the command was asked to process. It's a way of letting an administrator do something potentially scary in a slower, more deliberate and controlled fashion.

The -Verbose parameter is similar: if used, it gives a cmdlet or function the ability to display more information about what it's doing, as it's doing it. So rather than typing a command, hitting Return, and watching a blank screen while stuff is happening, an administrator can get some indication of what's happening "under the hood."

These are important functional concepts, because administrators aren't always in the best frame of mind when they're dealing with an emergency. Snover recalls:

I once spent a horrible week sleeping on the floor and eating out of vending machines at the Elvis Presley Memorial Trauma Center as my startup company's software (MUMPs) was used to develop a hospital records system and the beta was going VERY badly. I was field fixing code and repairing databases trying to make it all work. It was high stakes and a complete boof-a-rama. I remember in the middle of this mess, I was awoken from my slumber on the datacenter floor – I was completely zonked and had to stitch database records together. I remember seeing half of a record with the phrase "GSW Abdomin..." or Gunshot Wound and I had to find the other half of the record.

By the way—I had hospital administrators screaming at me because they had patients in hallways with IV bags that couldn't get procedures because of ME!

[Expletive deleted]

I remember thinking that it was insane that I was making such high impact decisions in a terrible state of mind with incomplete information.

Snover wanted PowerShell to be the tool that "had your back" when it was 3am, you were exhausted, but had to do high-impact things. So things like -Confirm, -WhatIf, and -Verbose were very "high value" for Snover and the team. And they achieved that value with very little code:

```
1   Function ShouldProcess(Object, Action)
2   {
3           If (Verbose)
4                   Write-Verbose "Doing ACTION on OBJECT"
5       Return TRUE
6           If (DEBUG)
7       Enter-Debugger()
8       Return TRUE
9           If (WHATIF)
10      Write-VERBOSE "WOULD have done ACTION on OBJECT"
11      Return FALSE
12          If (CONFIRM)
13      Write-VERBOSE "Do you want to ACTION on OBJECT y/n?"
14      If (Read-host == 'Y')
15          Return TRUE
16      Else
17          Return FALSE
18  }
```

The actual production code, Snover says, "is not much longer than this—it is one of the best 'value per lines of code' ever!" He adds, "I'm proud of that and feel so good that we provide these capabilities to admins to help them in their times of need."

Punctuation Decisions

Jim Truher was responsible for a lot of the decisions and compromises that inevitably happen when you're designing something like PowerShell. He recalls some of the things that he still gets grief over from the shell's fans.

Why is a backtick (grave accent) character used for line continuation and escape sequences? "A language that doesn't have a line continuation (or escape) character isn't much of a language, and I *sure* wasn't going to have an end-of-line like ";" be required—that would have probably killed interactive use entirely. I had started with the POSIX shell BNF and excised a bunch of stuff. I knew about "\" [as an escape character], of course, but sadly Windows had chosen that character as the directory separator—it was out. One of the things I removed was the backtick as a command substitution character, so it was freed up and I wasn't planning on using it for anything else. I considered a number of other things, but in the end I chose the backtick."

Why is the ‹ character still reserved by the shell? "I was going to keep › as redirect output and wanted its pair ‹. In our environment I thought it might be useful for things like...

```
do-something < file.txt
```

...which takes the contents of file.txt and inputs them to the Do-Something command. But in our environment it's just as easy to type...

```
Get-Content file.txt | do-something
```

...without much additional text. However, I thought it would be useful for those Unix guys whose muscle memory led them to type the former. I would still like to see it for completeness."

Why -eq as an equality operator instead of == like most languages use? "Huh, operators (here Jeffrey and I still disagree). I had convinced myself that the proper base was POSIX and its operators was the right model, mostly because it was in heavy use and was really our target customer. I did talk to a cshell proponent early on (there was one at Microsoft at the time), but it was really not something that was persuasive, especially if the parser needs to know the "mode" you're in if you want if (1 › 2) to work as expected. I also had a pretty solid idea that new operators [ones not present in traditional programming languages or shells] would be needed and I wanted some consistency with our operators. So, I stuck to my guns and now we have `-eq`, `-lt`, `-replace`, and so on. As an interesting aside, we actually supported `==` and `!=` for quite some time and pulled it late in the release cycle."

And what's with `::`? "So .NET allows you to have an instance and static member of the same name, and we couldn't disambiguate them with just `.`, so we needed a way to figure out which one to call. I mocked up a bunch of different sigils to see how they looked and felt and settled on `::` because it was still a dot (sort of—from a visual acuity perspective). By this time we were really running low on tokens [that were available for use]."

Snover says: "Jim's wrong. I'm right. :)"

He continues: "If there was anyway that we could have produced an unambiguous grammar by using C-style operators [such as `==`, `<`, `>`, and the like], I would have been very tempted to go against my conviction that Jim & Bruce own the language and jammed this one.

"One of the tensions here was the Principle of And: we wanted to be interactive *and* programmatic. We really wanted there to be a glide path between GUIs, PowerShell, and C#, which is why I *really* wanted C-style operators."

Snap-ins vs. Modules

PowerShell has two main models for adding cmdlets and other capabilities to the shell: PSSnapins and Modules. PSSnapins were released with v1.0, and continue to be supported in *Windows* PowerShell (but not the cross-platform "just PowerShell") today. Modules were introduced in v2.0, and remain the preferred means of extending the shell. But few people know that both modules *and* snap-ins were options for v1.0. The choice came down to politics.

Remember that, in terms of shipping-in-the-box Windows components, the Windows architects weren't fans of .NET. Snover recalls the "seven gates" that were ostensibly designed to ensure Windows could remain secure and stable, but in reality were basically a set of rules that .NET couldn't meet. Or so they thought: after Snover and team managed to clear the "seven gates," they recall discovering the "eighth gate," which was simply, "no .NET."

One of those hurdles was how PowerShell could be extended, and Snover proposed both snap-ins and modules. Two different Windows architects were involved in the decision, and predictably, they had two different preferences.

One preferred modules, because they could be "XCopy deployed." Xcopy.exe was one of Windows' long-time command-line tools, designed to copy entire directory trees of files from one place to another. An "XCopy deployment" was seen as low-impact, because you could "uninstall" the copied application by simply deleting its files. Another, however, preferred that add-ins register themselves in the Windows registry, which is what PSSnapins did. That way, Windows would be "aware" of the installation, and it would "know" where to go if a patch or other fix needed to be deployed.

"Which is it?" Snover asked.

"My way!" they *both* said.

So Snover did the political math. It basically came down to which of the two architects was likely to put up the biggest barricade to PowerShell's adoption, and that was the guy who preferred PSSnapins. So PSSnapins it was.

Incidentally, the name "snapins" was chosen because, at the time, Windows GUI administration was built around the Microsoft Management Console, or MMC. The MMC, as has been mentioned, was a general framework. Individual product teams would produce "snapins," which loaded into the MMC and provided administration for their products. By choosing the term "snapins," the PowerShell team hoped to present themselves as "just like the MMC," hopefully overcoming some objections from the Windows Architecture team. It didn't end up fooling anyone, but the name stuck.

Namespaces

Namespaces are an important part of many programming environments. For example, in PowerShell, the team reserves the use of "PS" for itself. That's why you don't have "snap-ins," you have *PSSnapins*. PowerShell v2 didn't technically introduce Remoting, it introduced *PSRemoting*. The PS creates a *namespace,* meaning a "space where all of the names are unique and related." In theory, someone might event some other kind of remote-control protocol. Let's say IBM did so. They might name their feature *IBMRemoting,* and have commands like `Enable-IBMRemoting`. That command could peacefully coexist with the `Enable-PSRemoting` command because the *namespace* portion of each command's name would make each one unique.

When Jeffrey Snover was working at Digital, he became the manager of an installation team. They had a software packaging and installation technology called SETLD that was, he says, "amazingly good, but had one critical flaw: package names could only be eight characters long." You might think that'd be enough, since it offers more than 2 trillion possible combinations, provided you're willing to deal with random-looking package names like "XKR7DJL8" or something. In reality, it can be fairly limiting. Each "product" that Snover's team worked with had multiple "packages," each needing a globally unique name. "It could only succeed if it failed," Snover says, meaning, "if people actually used it, you would quickly exhaust the namespace."

Snover wanted to make sure PowerShell didn't suffer from the same problem. First, PowerShell places no practical limits on the length of command names (examples like "Disable-Net Adapter Encapsulated Packet Task Offload" prove that point; in PowerShell that's typed without the spaces but it literally won't fit across a single line of text in this book), so that would be a help. But Snover stopped and asked the team, "what does success look like?" He broke it down:

1. How many cmdlets will there be in the industry overall?
2. How many cmdlets would a large customer have?
3. How many cmdlets would an individual admin use?

The answer to the first question was, "potentially *tens of thousands*," and so they needed a way to manage that vast namespace. Power-Shell's cmdlet names are based on a *verb-noun* pattern. You don't worry about the verbs overlapping; indeed, PowerShell defines a fairly limited set of verbs that you're supposed to use, in order to preserve consistency and protect users' learning investments. It's the nouns where things could go wrong. Imagine a noun like *Mailbox* as an example. Would that refer to a Microsoft Exchange Server mailbox? A Gmail mailbox? An IBM Domino mailbox? Some means of *disambiguation* was required.

But there's some subtlety there. Would a single customer ever be likely to use both Microsoft Exchange *and* Gmail? Probably not. So it's probably fine if both of those ship a cmdlet called "Get-Mailbox," because *within a single customer,* that "Mailbox" would only refer to one thing. But what about a noun like "User?" Most companies might have user accounts in Active Directory, perhaps in their SAP enterprise management system, maybe in some proprietary application—the term "User" could refer to a lot of distinct things, even within a single customer environment. So disambiguation would be needed.

The team's solution—to prepend a more-specific prefix to nouns—helped "divvy up" the broad global namespace. You'd have "Get-ActiveDirectoryUser" or "Get-ADUser," not just "Get-User." But that could get out of hand—hello, Disable-NetAdapterBlahBlahBlah—in terms of how much you had to type. So the team did some math and recommended that prefixes be 2-4 characters in length. It might not be *absolute* disambiguation, but it was something.

Unfortunately, a recommendation isn't an edict. Today, you see *lots* of PowerShell command names with long prefixes (like "NetAdapter"). But the team meant well.

Verbs

The team spent quite a long time coming up with the list of approved verbs for cmdlet names[6]. At Digital, Jeffrey admired the DIGITAL Command Language, or DCL, in part because it offered only limited verbs. You didn't have to wonder if a command started with "Create" or "New" because only one of those was a standard verb in DCL. That limited "verb space" made it easier to learn the product, and to apply what you'd learned elsewhere.

Snover and the team spent a lot of time identifying possible verbs, and boiling them all down to just one for any given intent. They decided on "Stop," and suggested that anyone considering using alternatives like "Kill," "Terminate," "End," and so on use the standard "Stop" instead.

Now the team had to decide if they'd *enforce* those standards, or merely *recommend* them.

Microsoft was, at the time, releasing a new Windows operating system every 3-5 years, and each release would have a 10-15 year real-world lifespan in customer environments. A concern with *enforcing* the "verb list" was, "if we get it wrong, we're going to be stuck with it for a looooong time." That could be a disaster. So the decision was to *recommend* the verb list, rather than *enforce* it. Meaning, PowerShell would grudgingly load up commands that

---

[6]The present list is at https://bit.ly/PowerShellVerbs, although that list represents an expansion since the v1 release.

had non-standard verbs in their names, rather than spewing an error and refusing to load them.

The team tried to work closely with partners both inside and outside Microsoft, to really promote proper verb usage. They wrote tons of documentation espousing best practices in verb selection. Then Citrix, one of the earlier companies other than Microsoft to produce a set of PowerShell commands for managing their products, came along. They released a set of commands with named like Citrix-GetUser and Citrix-GetMachine—definitely not following *any* of the practices the PowerShell team had been trying to spread around.

Snover's brain exploded.

PowerShell today still doesn't *enforce* proper verb usage. There's just a ton of risk in getting it wrong and breaking things for people. But it *does* now use a "shaming" approach: attempting to load a module that has unapproved verbs will result in a WARNING message. "Sadly," Snover says, "we didn't go with my suggested wording, which was something to the effect of, 'WARNING: you are using a snap-in produced by morons that don't care about you or your user experience.'"

Internally, Microsoft gently enforced proper verb usage by providing other teams with a tool called the "Cmdlet Designer." The Designer let you define all of your verbs and actions, and then produced code templates to help jump-start cmdlet development. It refused to accept unapproved verbs, and so became a good "nudge" for people to do the right thing. That tool was later released to the public, helping encourage those outside Microsoft to also do the right thing, verb-wise.

COM

As mentioned earlier, one of Microsoft's older component-software models, in use before .NET Framework was released, was Component Object Model, or COM. Although technically "deprecated" (meaning, it'll still work but don't make new investments in it) by .NET, tons of administrative functionality had already been written in COM. In keeping with Kenneth Hansen's "Principle of And," PowerShell would attempt to support .NET Framework *and* WMI *and* COM *and* anything else it could.

But COM would prove to be tricky.

Written in .NET, PowerShell is what Microsoft refers to as *managed code.* That means its code runs in a kind of sandbox, intended to help protect other system components from any bugs or failures. From within that sandbox, accessing .NET functionality is easy; "stepping outside" the sandbox and accessing COM was harder. .NET Framework itself provides a layer called *COM Interop,* intended to "adapt" COM into .NET as much as possible. But PowerShell still needed its own "COM adapter" in order to fully utilize COM.

Unfortunately, as the PowerShell team mapped feature desires to available resources, the COM adapter didn't make the cut. Software developer Arul Kumaravel, who'd been especially enthusiastic about the COM adapter and its value to the product, wasn't happy, but agreed that the other features were more important.

A few weeks before code lockdown in 2006, Arul approached Program Manager Hilal Al-Hilali and asked if the COM adapter could be included in the product if Arul coded it on his own time. Hilal explained that it wasn't just coding: there also needed to be testing, documentation, and so on. They debated for a while, and Hilal eventually agreed that Arul could work on the COM adapter if it didn't impact his other deliverables, or the deliverables of the test team. Given how close to lockdown they were, Hilal didn't think it would happen.

A couple of weeks later, Arul proudly presented the completed COM adapter, fully tested and documented.

"I don't know how he did it," Hilal says. "Maybe he had been working on it all along and just waited 'til the end, but it was good that it happened at the end so no one else got the idea that they could add features. It actually proved to be a useful addition to v1."

What's in a Name?

Why "PowerShell?"

Snover actually favored launching the product as Monad, although there's ample evidence that he had few supporters inside Microsoft. Even the beta releases in 2005 and 2006 hinted at a simple name like "Microsoft Shell," or MSH.

But there were lots more choices. Snover remembers "UniShell," "Unity," "OmniShell" (which Snover remembers liking) and even "Salt." (Two of those are names of completely different products, today, from companies other than Microsoft.)

So Marketing got involved, and proposed "PowerShell." Bob Muglia, in charge over all of Windows at the time, hated it. But, in the decision-making framework used by Microsoft, Marketing owned the decision on product names. After a bit of arguing, Marketing went out and did some "user research," listing several names—including PowerShell—and asking survey-takers "which name makes you feel more like you're getting a powerful shell?" A push-poll to be sure, and PowerShell won. Muglia admitted that Marketing did indeed "own the decision," and that he'd been wrong to press back so hard. PowerShell it was.

For what it's worth, a lot of the original Monad team didn't love the "PowerShell" name all that much either, with many of them pushing for "Microsoft Shell." There's a fun story there: "Microsoft Shell," as a name, basically died because it was *internally confusing* within Microsoft. Inside Microsoft, you see, the "shell" refers to the Graphical User Interface, or GUI, that you use to interact with the Windows operating system. The "shell" is the Start menu, the desktop icons, and so on. Jim Truher specifically advocated for "Microsoft Shell" in an effort to "take back" the word "shell," because, as he notes, "only at Microsoft would anyone ever consider a GUI to be a 'shell.'"

Interestingly, there was *already* a PowerShell out there. It's hard to find references to it today, but the first PowerShell was an open-source, Linux-based command-line shell. Microsoft contacted its author, and they decided that since Microsoft's product was *Windows* PowerShell, it'd be fine. Today, that Linux shell is pretty much forgotten (it never had broad adoption anyway), and today's cross-platform shell from Microsoft is known simply as "PowerShell."

Remoting and Buffering

As PowerShell users know, the shell's engine provides a great deal of built-in functionality that add-in cmdlets get "for free." Exception handling, pipeline control, and so on are all built in.

When we think about PowerShell's pipeline, we often think of a command like this:

```
1  Get-Process |
2  Where CPUUsage -gt .9 |
3  Sort Name |
4  Format-Table
```

In theory, the Get-Process command runs until it produces an object into the pipeline. That object is then passed to the Where(-Object) command, which either passes the object along or discards it. Passed-along objects are then sent to the Sort(-Object) command, which you would expect to "save them all up" until it has all the objects, can sort them into order, and then place them into the pipeline to the next command.

In reality, though, PowerShell was *designed* to run across remote computers. In *theory*, the Get-Process command could be running on one node, while the Where(-Object) command ran *on a completely different node.* Passing objects onto the network one-by-one could result in a lot of unnecessary network traffic, making PowerShell "chatty" and diminishing network performance: each object would require a certain amount of fixed overhead to create, manage, and disconnect each session.

So PowerShell includes a buffering system that's part of the "free" functionality provided to each cmdlet. The business of "each command could be running on a different node" never really came to the level of fruition the designers originally imagined, but the functionality is still there, in the often-overlooked -OutBuffer common parameter. This parameter lets you indicate how many objects should be "buffered" before they're all output to the pipeline. By default, it's basically 1, meaning there is no buffering.

This feature has a bit of a story of its own. The developer in charge of it and some other features kept dropping it from his to-do list. Kenneth Hansen, during status meetings, would continually ask, "where's buffering?" and the developer would reply, "oh, right," and put it back on. This happened several times before Hansen—normally the very definition of a calm, collected professional—sort of lost it and started yelling. The developer shot back with, "well, this'll take six weeks—do you still want it?" That created a bit of a quiet moment: PowerShell was already behind schedule at that point, and six weeks is a long time. Hansen consulted with Snover. "Six weeks?" Snover said. "That's ridiculous." So Snover proceeded to code the output buffering himself—in thirteen lines of code.

"Oh," the developer replied when confronted with it. "You wanted to do it *that* way."

Updatable Help

PowerShell v1 shipped with an extensive set of help files for its over 100 pre-loaded cmdlets. The intent was to provide a rich set of documentation and examples that people could use to get started, and it worked well. PowerShell was famously one of the few shells ever made to have such a consistent and extensive out-of-the-box help experience. But it also created a problem.

Microsoft documentation has to be translated into over a dozen different languages, to support the company's users across the world. As a result, the documentation files have to be "locked down" significantly ahead of any release date, to allow time for translation. The help files were, in fact, "locked down" long before the code itself was locked down for shipping. As a result, ongoing changes to the code often wound up conflicting with the help files, because the help files couldn't be updated in time.

"Well," you might think, "just ship new help files." Great idea— except that by PowerShell v2.0, *PowerShell was a component of the Windows operating system.* The only way you "ship updates" to Windows is via the Windows Update patch process. Enterprise administrators do *not* want to be told that "Patch Tuesday"—a major part of most organizations' IT planning cycles—is going to consist of a bunch of help files! Microsoft actually wound up wasting *millions* of dollars shipping "bad" help files, with no easy way to update them after the fact.

So a later version of PowerShell shipped with *no* help, and instead introduced "updatable help." By running an Update-Help command, the shell would scan all of its installed modules and snap-ins, check each one to see if help files were available online, and then download and install those help files. Because the files weren't shipped *with* the operating system, they could be downloaded outside the Windows Update patch cycles. It also meant that the company could hold off on "documentation lockdown" until much closer to release dates, release English help first, and later make translated files available for download.

Today, PowerShell has shifted to an open-source model for help files. They're written in the Markdown markup format, and stored in a public GitHub repository. A set of tools automate the process of turning Markdown into both the XML-based format PowerShell uses natively for help, as well as HTML files that can be published on Microsoft's documentation websites. Best of all, anyone can contribute to the help files by submitting pull requests in GitHub.

The Directed Graph

Snover had big thoughts for PowerShell. It was designed from the get-go as an object-flow engine. So if you have the command:

```
1  A | B | C
```

You run "A" until it produces an object, which is sequenced to "B" and then "C." This is a directed graph[7], which is a fairly high-end mathematical term that, if you oversimplify it to death, means "doing things in a sequence." This is distinct from a directed acyclic graph[8], in which A might pipe something directly to C. But the system was always designed to support cycles.

In v1.0, the team acknowledged that they were building a dis-tributed automation engine, with only one flow-through. But, the team said, we'll have various streams of data. In addition to the main pipeline, there'll be a stream for errors, one for verbose output, one for debug output, one for warnings, and so on. All of those could then create additional sequences for processing sets of objects. We'll figure out other interfaces for this down the line, they

---

[7]https://en.wikipedia.org/wiki/Directed_graph
[8]https://en.wikipedia.org/wiki/Directed_acyclic_graph

thought—think of the uses for monitoring, distributed management, and so on.

But Snover screwed up. While he wasn't paying attention, one of the key developers basically hardcoded the PowerShell engine to presume the use of a command-line interface. That took all those other scenarios off the table, and by the time anyone realized, it was too late. Rolling back and starting over would have been demonstrably expensive, whereas the value of those vaguely imagined other interfaces wasn't clear. So it never came to be.

White on Blue

Windows PowerShell's default color scheme has always been white text on a dark blue background. That wasn't, as you might think, some ad-hoc decision made in a hallway by a couple of developers. No, actual *usability testing* was conducted to find an appropriate color scheme that provided good contrast, good readability, and good long-term comfort. Sadly, the usability folks missed the low-contrast red-on-black color scheme used for error messages!

Windows PowerShell's command-line host was built around the same Windows Console application that housed the old, MS-DOS-style Cmd.exe shell. That application had a specific set of color options, and so the team had to pick from those. Today, the cross-platform PowerShell runs as an application *within native terminal windows,* rather than "owning" its own window. It also defaults to using the PSReadLine module to provide more powerful input, coloring, and other features. For that reason, modern users of PowerShell (versus Windows PowerShell) get to control their own default color schemes, and even customize the colors used by PSReadLine.

Creating a Language

"Lingua, 'Ōlelo, Idioma, Språk..."

There is perhaps no human better able to discuss PowerShell's language than Bruce Payette. Hired into the original "Kermit" team, Payette also had a strong Unix background and had worked in Microsoft's Services for Unix team.

"I'm glad that we brought Bruce on," Daryl Wray remembered, "because honestly, we had nobody with language expertise. Developing a language is quite a unique endeavor. We were able to defer to Bruce's expertise on that quite largely, and you know, I think that led to a pretty approachable [product]."

Wray did note that he had invented the word *cmdlet,* pronounced, "command-let," which refers to the commands that live natively inside of PowerShell. At the time, he said, the documentation folks gave him some grief for it, because they hated inventing new words. As it turns out, the use of *cmdlet* was a blessing. Add it to any Google search, for example, and you automatically limit your results to those relating to PowerShell, because PowerShell is the only place *cmdlet* is a word.

But back to the language: Snover may have created the idea for what the shell would address, and how it would act, but it was critical that the team find a way for human beings to tell the shell what to actually *do.* PowerShell is similar to a programming language in that way, in that you use its *language* to tell the shell what steps to take, in what order to take them, and so on. Developing new computer languages from scratch is tricky: designers often like to borrow concepts from existing languages, but PowerShell was a bit of a unique situation. It wasn't *intended* for computer programmers: it was intended for computer *administrators.* That means certain programming approaches that a programmer might take for granted might be alien to an administrator. PowerShell's language needed to be *powerful,* but it also needed to be simple and *approachable,* or admins would ignore it.

At PowerShell + DevOps Global Summit 2018, Payette gave a talk[9] on some of the history of PowerShell's language and architecture. One key point Payette makes early in the talk is that, while Power-Shell needed to be easy for a sophisticated user, it also needed to recognize that everyone would have to *learn* PowerShell. Learning, he says, "is hard, and so we need to facilitate it and *protect it.*" That last bit—protecting learning—is a critical part of The PowerShell ethos that a lot of people overlook or misunderstand. Much of the

---

[9]https://bit.ly/PayetteLanguageTalk

consistency in PowerShell—particularly in the core commands and language, if not the commands written by others—comes from that desire to protect users' learning investment.

Payette also points out the unusual tension that PowerShell would need to deal with. Traditionally, systems administrators have relied on what Payette terms "whipitupitude," or the ability to quickly "pull something out of your ass" to get a job done. That's an important need, especially since administrators are often *reacting* to circumstances rather than *planning* their actions. But "whipping something up" doesn't always create solutions with the stability and staying power that businesses require, which is why "real" programming languages tend to be deeply structured, forcing programmers into "doing the right thing" as much as possible. PowerShell needed to do *both*, enabling quick, ad-hoc solutions as well as leading its users to sustainable, stable, maintainable coding practices.

Payette describes a number of PowerShell's "Big Ideas." One of those was the use of a *domain-specific vocabulary*, meaning the *words* used by PowerShell were limited and fixed (albeit not actually enforced in the first version). The vocabulary was designed to limit the amount someone would have to learn, and again, to *protect* that learning investment.

Another big idea takes a bit of explanation. Traditionally, command-line shells don't do any *parsing* of commands. For example, suppose you sat down at a Linux computer, opened a terminal window, and entered sudo chown -R system /etc/data. The shell would simply run the sudo command, and give it everything else you'd typed. The sudo command, in turn, would run the chown command, and pass along everything else from that line of text. Each command is responsible for its own *parsing,* or deciding what to do with the information you've given it. That approach makes it fairly nontrivial to write new commands. Although templates and libraries exist to make the workload a little easier, each command's author has a significant amount of work to do, and significant control over what you end up having to learn in order to use their command.

PowerShell would be different. It would offer *universal parsing*. When you run Get-CimInstance -Class Win32_Process -Computer REMOTE, the shell itself is figuring out that you want to run a command called Get-CimInstance, and that you're providing two pieces of input information. If you provided those pieces in a different order, or you used a shortcut (-Computer instead of -ComputerName), or whatever, the *shell* would figure that out. The actual Get-CimInstance command would be handed your input information in a standardized format, meaning the author of the command would have a lot less work to do. It would therefore be easier for people to write PowerShell commands, since a big chunk of the "dirty work" was being done for them in a consistent and reliable fashion.

PowerShell also took another burden off of command authors' backs: parameter checking. Traditionally, a command author has to check every single piece of information you feed the command, to ensure they're all valid. For example, run ping 192.16.0.12 -n 100, the ping command has to internally validate that 100 is a valid entry for the -n parameter. PowerShell would offer to make that easier, by allowing command authors to declare a set of rule for what *was* valid input. PowerShell itself would execute those rules, and if the user provided invalid input, PowerShell would produce the appropriate error messages. Again, less work for the command author and more consistency for the user. Of course, it didn't always work out: comments right in PowerShell's source code, dating back to 2004, indicate instances where declarative parameter constraints went "deeply wrong" in instances that the team simply hadn't foreseen.

Now to the actual language of PowerShell.

While PowerShell does enable the ad-hoc, whip-something-up functionality administrators expect of a shell, Microsoft knew it needed to also supply a simple, robust scripting language. A scripting language is a kind of "lightweight" programming language that lends itself well to administrative automation. Scripting languages usually contain basic decision-making constructs ("if the user is in the management group, give them the following permissions"), looping constructs ("perform the following on every file in this folder"), and so on.

PowerShell was *originally conceived* as having a "pluggable" scripting language. In other words, the *shell* and the *language* would be separate, interchangeable parts. Don't like the stock language? Swap it in for another one! As PowerShell was developed, though, the engine and the language became more deeply intertwined. For example, the engine *uses* the language in its formatting subsystem, and the Extensible Type System can use elements of the scripting language to construct new methods and properties. As the two became more closely interdependent, the idea of a pluggable scripting language was set aside.

PowerShell's language—unsurprisingly, if you remember what Kermit was designed to do—started largely with the POSIX.2 shell grammar, which was essentially the Unix KornShell scripting language. Big implementation changes had to be made for PowerShell, but some of the roots of POSIX are visible today:

- Variables that start with $
- Subexpressions like $(Get-Something)
- Connecting commands to one another using the | pipe character

And so on. Team members' experience with the Digital Equipment Company (DEC) Control Language (DCL) are also evident, including the Command-Name -parameter: value pattern that all PowerShell commands use today.

For other things the team knew they needed, neither POSIX nor DCL provided ready-made inspiration. In those cases, they turned to the Perl language, which was popular on Unix and Linux for its string-parsing prowess, and which in the early 2000s was the dominant scripting language of the Internet. It offered arrays, hash tables, and regular expressions, all of which the team knew they wanted in PowerShell. The use of @( ) to designate an array, for example, is straight out of Perl. Perl's contribution to PowerShell gets a bit lost, because so many other languages have *also* been inspired by Perl. It's easy to look at PowerShell and see evidence linking back to PHP, for example, but Perl was an original inspiration for that, too.

In the end though, Payette said, "Perl is kind of icky as a language." Perl evolved from a shell background, but it never rethought itself fresh. The team didn't want to just slavishly copy something—if you're okay with doing that, why not just use the original thing to begin with? So while some of Perl's syntax elements live on in PowerShell, the team made a deliberate shift to a C#-style structure. The language structure of C# closely aligns, to some extent or another, to a huge number of other C-derived languages: C++, Java, Go, Objective-C, and more. It's as close to a "universal syntax model" as anything in the computer world, and the shift offered another putative advantage: PowerShell would look like Microsoft's C# language. C# programmers would be able to pick up PowerShell more easily, and PowerShell users would have a "glide path," in Jeffrey Snover's words, to C#.

Payette describes a key different between PowerShell and almost all other shells, using the phrase *expand and parse.* Most shells take something you've typed:

```
cp $source 'output.txt'
```

And they *expand* that one line, filling in variables' contents and other tasks to form a complete command line:

```
cp 'input.txt' 'output.txt'
```

They then *parse* the line, figuring out which bits are the command name, which bits are arguments, and so on:

```
1   Command: cp
2   Argument 1: 'input.txt'
3   Argument 2: 'output.txt'
```

Then they run the command, passing in whatever arguments. PowerShell doesn't follow that behavior, though. Instead, it parses *the entire script,* constructing (since v3) an Abstract Syntax Tree which is then executed. There are advantages to this approach, but one disadvantage pops up frequently with Unix and Linux users who are trying PowerShell for the first time: PowerShell's command aliases—the ability to type something like `gci` instead of the full `Get-ChildItem` command name—are *static.* In Linux, an alias can have dynamic elements that are evaluated while they're run; with PowerShell, aliases can only point to a command name, because they need to be able to resolve to something concrete when the script is parsed.

Trivia: PowerShell supports something called *splatting,* which is where you load a command's arguments into a sort of array, and then just pass that array:

```
1   $args = @{input='in.txt'
2              output='out.txt'
3              method=5}
4   Do-Command @args
```

PowerShell uses the @ character when splatting the variable, which makes "splatting" seem like an odd word. The concept, though, comes from Ruby, which uses the * character. If you imagine the * as what you'd get if you *splatted* a bug onto a piece of paper, the word make a tiny bit more sense!

Language design decisions like this can go on seemingly forever. After all, when you're creating something new, there are a lot of questions to answer! Should we use this:

```
1  Get-Something -argument $value
```

Or this:

```
1  Get-Something /argument $value
```

Unix *tends* to use the dash, or a double dash, because the forward-slash is a file system path separator. Since Windows was "competing" with Unix, the team opted for the dash.

Not everyone was pleased with how PowerShell's language was being designed, though. Jim Truher remembers having "a bunch of people push back on our language. The syntax we were building had *way* more than was needed for the simple admin scenarios we had talked about (especially if you compared it to Cmd.exe). I knew that languages 'find their own level' and that we if we built something expressive enough, it would find its own place in the world (and I wanted that to be *far* more than just administration scenarios)

"From my perspective, I wanted something that I could use to match my experience on Unix. If it didn't do that it wouldn't have the ability to get very far and only be this niche app for small things and wouldn't survive.

"I wanted to make it expressive enough to break out of the 'administration tool' box it [started] in. It was the guerrilla approach to product creation: publicly suggest that it was appropriate for a smaller task, when in reality it was good for so much more.

"I think now that I'm really glad folks weren't paying closer attention, otherwise they would have seen the broader reach we would have and we would have been squashed."

Snover agrees: "Right – we put Bruce and Jim in charge of the language. Other people had opinions but we set things up so that Jim and Bruce were the owners of the language—full stop.

"There was a hilarious story where the engineering manager (the one that almost killed Jim on Ctrl+C) came to me and asked who should get credit for the language.

"I told her that Jim and Bruce did.

"She wanted to know who did the bulk of the work.

"I said that they were jointly responsible, Program Manager and Developer working together—a textbook example of how we want everyone to work.

"Yea but if someone was going to get 51% credit – which one would it be?"

"I did not answer that question—I stood fast that they both get 100% credit."

The Security Story

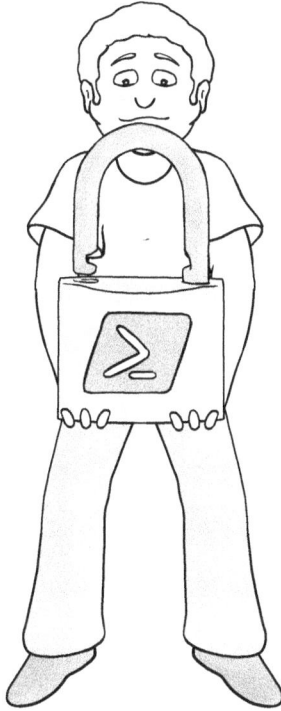

From the outset, the deck was stacked against PowerShell when it came to security. Not because of anything in PowerShell itself, but because of its predecessors.

Visual Basic Scripting Edition, or VBScript, was an administrator's go-to automation language for Windows operating systems in the early 2000s, and it had a less-than-stellar security story. As with most security stories, only part of the problem was VBScript itself;

the rest was firmly on the shoulders of its users.

VBScript, with its ease of use, relatively low learning curve, broad access to the underlying Windows internals, and ubiquity across Windows operating systems, simply became a popular way to write computer viruses and other attacks. Mind you, a virus creator could have chosen to use a number of other languages—C++, for example, or even C#—but those language required you to compile your program into an executable, or EXE, file. Sending an EXE file as an email attachment, hoping the recipient would double-click it and execute it, wasn't easy. Many users were aware of what an EXE file was, and many organizational security measures—like anti-virus applications—specifically blocked EXE file attachments. VBScript files, on the other hand, were often allowed through. At least in the beginning; eventually, people caught on and blocked those as well.

But public perception can be blurry, especially on technical topics. Visual Basic for Applications (VBA), vaguely related to VBScript, was embedded in productivity applications like Microsoft Word, Microsoft Excel, and so on. So virus authors pivoted, porting their VBScript-based malware into "VBA Macros" embedded within innocent-looking Word or Excel documents. Users were accustomed to double-clicking *those* as attachments, and so "Visual Basic as a malware entry point" became even more prevalent. Some of the most epic Windows-targeting malware of the age came via VBScript and VBA, carrying cute names like "Melissa" and "ILoveYou."

All of that baggage was set firmly at PowerShell's doorstep, as it was positioned to be the new, installed-on-every-desktop-and-server scripting language to succeed VBScript. PowerShell hadn't even been finished yet, and people were already talking about the "Monad Virus" after someone on the Internet coded up a PowerShell-based proof-of-concept virus.

That's the environment in which Lee Holmes came to the PowerShell team. Lee would, over the years, become famous for his advocacy for security, his methodical approach to the topic, and his pushing for ever-smarter security within the core PowerShell engine and its supporting elements. And before it was all over, much of the security thought and engineering that went into PowerShell wound up impacting Windows, and even other shells and operating systems, in a hugely positive way.

Holmes came to Microsoft right out of university, as a software engineer on the Microsoft Encarta team. For those of you too young to remember, Encarta was Microsoft's online multimedia encyclopedia, and Lee was working on security and authorization aspects of the product. He saw a rumor on Slashdot, based upon a leaked job description from Microsoft, that the company was developing a new command-line shell. So he did some internal digging, and ran across Monad as it was just getting out of its earliest prototype stages. Holmes came from a Unix background, and so the idea of a powerful command-line shell intrigued him. He introduced the shell to Encarta's operations team, whom he'd been occasionally helping with various projects, and Holmes says it "became obvious" that the new shell would be a game-changer for Microsoft and the industry.

So Holmes made a case, went through the interview loop, and found himself a job as a Software Engineer on the "Monad" team, working primarily on security. At the time, the team had one developer loosely working on security stuff, but the product was still so early-days that no much had been done, giving Holmes a more or less blank slate. At that point, two of PowerShell's v1 security features had already been finished or roughed in.

First up was script signing, the ability to add a cryptographic signature to a script that would identify the script's author, and guarantee that the script hadn't been changed since it had been signed by the author. This had long been a staple of software security, and was even available in the VBScript world. Making Windows itself understand that a particular file type—in this case, the text-based .PS1 files that were PowerShell scripts—could be signed was a big task. A lot of the work that went into that wound up being re-used elsewhere across Windows to secure other file types.

Second was PowerShell's Execution Policy, which controls which kinds of scripts that can run on a computer. Execution Policy is an often-misunderstood feature, because it requires you to really take a step back and define your security boundary. For example, some companies will say things like, "we don't want our administrators to be able to screw up the environment by running a badly written script." That's a bad security boundary, though. Your administrators already have all the ability they need to screw up the environment, with or without PowerShell; you either need to find a way to trust them, or take away their administrator abilities.

That kind of high-level thinking was where the team started: who are we trying to protect against? What actions are we trying to prevent? What are our guiding principles? For the most part, that kind of discussion had never been had about a scripting language or shell before, even in the Linux and Unix worlds. People tend to jump to binary questions like "is this secure or not?" but security isn't ever a binary answer, and "secure" is not an absolute, objective term. For example, if an attacker has compromised a computer, and obtained administrator privileges, and are about to use PowerShell as their last stage in deploying their attack, then PowerShell is not your security problem. Your security problem started much earlier, and if you'd been thinking about your security boundaries in the right way, you'd realize that.

PowerShell Remoting, introduced in v2.0, is a good example. A lot of organizations have a knee-jerk reaction to Remoting, and simply disable it. That's typically because the security decision-maker isn't educated about Remoting or its alternatives, and they're making an uninformed decision. For example, you *could* simply disconnect all the computers from the network, and you'd be *very* secure, but you'd also be non-operational as an organization!

As administrators manage ever-growing numbers of computers—often in the thousands—they *need* the ability to manage them remotely. Many organizations would "standardize" on Microsoft's Remote Desktop Protocol, or RDP, which enables an administrator to remotely log into a remote computer's graphical user interface (GUI) and perform administrative actions. But here's the catch: the RDP protocol *transmits that administrator's credentials across the network,* so that the remote computer can "log them in." If you have a thousand computers, the odds are *one* of them will eventually be compromised in some way, and your administrator credentials will be gifted to some attacker via RDP. Remoting, on the other hand, was *designed* with those attacks in mind. Remoting by default *never* transmits credentials across the network. An *informed* security decision-maker would take the time to understand that, and the ones who do often disable RDP and insist on using Remoting instead.

Security, in other words, is complex. It's deeply technical, and it takes time to understand and make decisions about.

Holmes was a primary driver behind the AMSI, or Anti-Malware Scan Interface, a part of Windows PowerShell that very few people even know exists. Today, it's a standard part of the Windows operating system, used by almost all major anti-malware vendors' products.

Back in the VBScript days, most anti-malware products used *file signatures* to detect malicious VBScript files and block them from running. A file signature usually looks at the file size, filename, a cryptographic hash of the file's contents, and so on, all intended to uniquely identify files. As new malicious scripts were discovered, vendors would add their signatures to their products, enabling their products to stop those scripts in the future.

Attackers hit back with *obfuscation,* a way of taking a script and encoding it in various ways, so that the script looked different to the anti-malware engines. So a single malicious script could suddenly have a thousand different appearances, making it difficult for engines to detect them all.

The anti-malware vendors' riposte was to implement their own VB-Script parsers and pseudo-runtimes. Basically, they'd try to "run" the script only to the point where VBScript had to de-obfuscate it, and they'd create signatures based on that final result. That worked, but it became a huge performance drain on lower-end computers. And the attackers hit back again: they'd look for vulnerabilities in those VBScript parsers and pseudo-runtimes, and write scripts specifically to exploit them, crash the anti-malware software, and then launch the "real" attack.

AMSI moves some of the attack points. Essentially, when Power-Shell runs a script, it first has to de-obfuscate the script, parse it into a set of tokens and such that its engine understands, and perform other tasks to get the script "set up" to actually execute. It does so, and *then* passes the result to AMSI. Anti-malware engines register to receive notices from AMSI, enabling them to examine the final, de-obfuscated, ready-to-run script to see if it matches one of their signatures for a malicious script. This is *much* harder to mess with, and it eliminates the need for a half-dozen different anti-malware vendors to have to come up with their own PowerShell parsers and stuff. PowerShell does what it knows how to do, and interfaces with the anti-malware products to let them do what *they* know how to do.

It wasn't a smooth path to get AMSI running. The Windows Defender team, responsible for Windows' built-in anti-malware software, weren't initially interested. So Holmes went on what he calls a "walking tour of campus," presenting his idea to different teams. He finally happened on one developer who'd worked on an existing Windows API, which was designed to hand email attachments off to anti-malware engines prior to opening those attachments. The two worked together, got the right other teams involved, and AMSI finally came to life. Today, *any* scrip language runtime on Windows can leverage AMSI to do the same thing. As this book is being written, AMSI is stopping around 10 million infections *per month.*

Command-line logging is another Windows feature that Power-Shell contributed to. In a nutshell, this feature creates an event log entry each time a new process is started, including the complete set of commands used to start the process. It's off by default, because a lot of process-starting commands include sensitive information like passwords. You certainly don't want that going into an event log where anyone—potentially even an attacker—can see them! PowerShell goes a step further with *protected* event logging. It uses an encryption certificate, which organizations install on their computers, to encrypt the event information prior to logging it. The company can then use decryption certificates—stored elsewhere—to view that information as needed. It's a Windows-wide feature, meaning any application can tap into it, and it's a pretty innovative approach to solving the problem.

Like anyone who's excited about their work, Holmes was eager to talk about it in public. The problem is that most of the major security conferences, with names like Defcon and Black Hat, really prefer to talk about *attacks.* Security exploits are sexy; stopping exploits is "meh." So Holmes' proposals to give talks on the security improvements in PowerShell were all turned down. But a new opportunity arose as the team started really getting their Just Enough Administration, or JEA, features polished up. In their current implementation, a few lines of configuration information enables JEA to lock down PowerShell so hard that it'll only do the *exact* tasks you permit, and only for the *specific* people you define. It's a huge security "win," and Holmes wanted to talk about it.

The official line is that the big security conferences are about *defending* against attacks. The reality is that presentations almost always spend 95% of their time on the attack itself, and then have one slide at the end with some generic advice about defending against it. Exploits are sexy; defending not so much. But Holmes decided to flip the script, proposing a provocatively titled session called, "Attacking a Battle-Hardened Windows Server." He spent two minutes on the "attack," and then twenty minutes talking about how JEA could be used to defend against it. The session was accepted, and became one of the first *defensive* PowerShell talks at a major security conference.

PowerShell's security story continues to evolve, as all good security stories should. PowerShell was the first command-line shell where security was part of the conversation up-front, and the first to have had a persistent, year-to-year investment in security improvements. No attack has been leveled against PowerShell that hasn't also been leveled against Unix shells for four decades, but PowerShell sits on over a billion computers running Windows, and so the security focus for PowerShell has to be commensurate with that attack surface. The team focused on security from the outset, and continues to do so, in one of PowerShell's most continually evolving aspects.

Greatest Misses

Not everything goes according to plan. Sometimes, a group of brilliant people can come up with a brilliant idea, but it still doesn't land the way they'd hoped. This is a chapter of PowerShell's greatest misses: the things that had held such hope, and just fell flat.

MiniShells and AdminShells

One of PowerShell v1's interesting—and to some, weird and misleading—concepts was the *minishell,* originally referred to as *adminshells.* Essentially, a minishell was a combination of the PowerShell engine, a specific set of PSSnapIns that contained cmdlets and/or Providers, all compiled into a single executable (EXE) file.

Minishells were intended to solve two problems. First, they were designed to address the Windows Architecture team's concerns about versioning. By distributing a minishell—say, one that included all the Exchange Server cmdlets—you created a *statically linked* application. That is, everything the application needed to run was right there within the application itself. If you'd written your cmdlets to work with PowerShell v1, then the v1 engine was embedded right within your app. You didn't have to worry about what might happen if your cmdlets were installed on a system running PowerShell v2, v3, or something else. Your minishell wasn't *dynamically linked* to whatever version of PowerShell was installed system-wide; instead, it simply used whatever version you'd compiled it with.

Importantly, *nothing stopped you from loading those Exchange cmdlets into a "normal" PowerShell instance.* That is, you could pop open "regular" PowerShell, run Add-PSSnapin, and go to town, ignoring the minishell completely.

Second, minishells *didn't allow you to add any other cmdlets to them.* The Add-PSSnapin cmdlet was effectively disabled (this was in v1, so modules weren't an option). The idea here was to make technical support easier. "I'm having trouble with my Exchange cmdlets!" you might cry out to Microsoft technical support. The job of technical support, during troubleshooting, is to eliminate as many potential causes for problems as possible. Rather than asking you, "okay, did you also load any other snapins that might be causing a conflict?" they would simply say, "open the Exchange minishell and let's start from there." They knew the minishell represented a "clean" environment, free from potential non-Microsoft issues.

For the public, minishells didn't go over well. The whole promise of PowerShell was to bring all of your administrative tools together in one place; minishells defeated that. You could open the Exchange minishell in one window, and the SQL Server minishell in another window, but you couldn't share functionality between them. Smart folks basically ignored the minishells, opened a regular PowerShell window, and loaded all the snapins they wanted into that one shell session.

Minishells also created confusion. The existence of the Exchange Management Shell icon on Windows' Start menu (which was technically not a minishell at all; it was a regular PowerShell instance that simply auto-loaded the Exchange snapin for you) implied that each Microsoft product would have to have its own "PowerShell." Newcomers didn't grasp that you *could* load all of your snapins into a single PowerShell window if you felt like it; they thought you'd wind up with a dozen different "PowerShells."

In the end, the SQL Server team was the only one that wound up shipping an actual minishell (and frankly, the SQL Server team developed something of an early reputation for kind of going their own way with regards to PowerShell). Other teams—like Exchange Server—would often create a Start menu icon that opened up "regular" PowerShell and pre-loaded their snapins, but even that practice faded away in the v2 timeframe as more and more products implemented PowerShell support.

Minishells technically exist today, in that developers can still create them in *Windows* PowerShell, but they're largely forgotten. In PowerShell—the cross-platform v6 and later product—snapins aren't a thing at all, and modules are the exclusive way of extending the shell. Minishells therefore became end-of-life with Windows PowerShell v5.1.

Transactions

Transactions are an important part of many computing systems. Think of computer transactions just like you would think of a transaction at your bank. Say you're cashing a check: your bank has to debit the amount from the originating account, and then credit that amount in your account. Both of those tasks must be accomplished successfully in order for the *transaction* to succeed. If something goes wrong—say, the originating account doesn't have enough money in it—then the *entire* transaction has to fail. It's all-or-nothing; you can't have just one task succeed.

Database systems have had transactions going back into computing's furthest history. They're considered a staple of database computing, and they're a reliable way to ensure the integrity of multi-task operations. Windows' file system and registry have also long supported transactions: you could, for example, have a transaction that required one file to be created, another to be deleted, and a third to be renamed, and ensure that all three tasks either succeeded or failed as a set. If one task failed, the file system could "roll back" the others, leaving the system in its original state.

Despite their long-standing presence in Windows, the transaction file system and registry features are fairly obscure and very rarely used. But it's a powerful concept, and one the PowerShell team decided to expose. The team went to great lengths to try and make the concept of transactions—which is somewhat abstract to most people—easy to understand and to use. "What if you could make a bunch of risky changes that required coordination," Lee Holmes remembers, "and know by the end of your script that they either all succeeded – or you were back to a clean slate?"

PowerShell accesses Windows' file system and registry through a PSProvider, meaning both are accessed through a single, common layer of code. In theory, that made adding transactional support straightforward, since the team only had to add it in one place, and then update those to Providers to behave accordingly. But the team decided to stay focused, and so they worked on the registry provider first. "This was a cross-company effort that involved the PowerShell team, folks behind the Distributed Transaction Coordinator team at Microsoft, and more," Holmes recalls.

"It was the thud heard around the world," he says.

Administrators struggled to find real-world scenarios where they'd use transactions, struggled to understand the concept, and in the end, simply didn't use the feature.

Workflow

In computing terms, a *workflow,* conceptually, is the idea of running a series of tasks. Those tasks might take a long time to complete, and they might even need to pause and resume so that the computer could restart itself midway through. Or they might need to "survive" a power failure, automatically resuming when power was restored. In the Monad Manifesto, the idea of workflows was the third major milestone Snover had identified.

Lee Holmes says, "When PowerShell was first gaining acceptance, the concept of 'Workflows' and 'Workflow Automation' were also gaining popularity. People would show these five or ten boxes [each representing a task], with lines and arrows [connecting] them, and just shine with glee at the idea that you could start to add some structure to business processes." It's a concept that's alive and well, often working under names like *runbook automation,* or *robotic process automation,* and other related terms.

He continues, "These really hit a sweet spot for extremely high-level business concepts, but like all things it made sense for Microsoft to start to support this at the technology level so everybody didn't need to implement their own workflow engine. The .NET team started adding support for these kind of systems through the Windows Workflow Foundation set of APIs."

Windows Workflow Foundation, or WWF, wound up being a major release feature for one of .NET Framework's versions, along with other new frameworks like Windows Presentation Foundation and Windows Communication Foundation. The idea was to provide a "base layer engine" that all other Microsoft Teams—as well as Microsoft's customers—could leverage.

"It wasn't long before the PowerShell team started hearing the pressure: 'PowerShell doesn't support workflows, so it's really not the technology for us.' What those folks were really looking for was automation and not workflows, they just didn't know it yet. But the clamor just kept getting louder, so we embarked on adding Workflows to PowerShell in a huge way [for v3]. We added a server role to maintain these long-running workflows. We generated tens of thousands of lines of code to expose PowerShell cmdlets as independent workflow 'Activities' [inside WWF]. We even wrote an entire compiler to statically analyze the data flow in scripts as had never been done before, and used this data to convert the PowerShell language into the XML-based description used for [WWF] workflows."

It was a tricky situation. The team enabled PowerShell users to create function-like Workflow constructs, which PowerShell would "translate" into the XML that WWF used. As a PowerShell user, a Workflow *looked* almost identical to a function. That was meant to be a good thing: protecting your learning investment and letting you leverage what you'd learned elsewhere. Writing a workflow was meant to be basically the same as writing a function. Except it *wasn't*. Workflows were their own beast, and there were long lists of exceptions for where workflows and functions differed. Core PowerShell concepts like variable scope worked differently, although it *looked* like it didn't. Workflows were confusing, because they weren't really running "in" PowerShell: you'd write something that *looked* PowerShell-y, but it would actually be executed by an engine with a completely different set of rules.

"I screwed up workflows," Snover admits. "100% my fault and one of the things I still feel terrible about."

"Lee (and others) produced a design which was great, and if we had gone with it—I'm sure that everyone would be using workflows today," he continues. "But we had the Common Engineering Criteria (CEC), and the CEC required using .NET workflows, not what Lee and the others had designed. Now, *many* teams were blowing off the CEC and doing whatever they wanted, whenever they wanted. BUT... [PowerShell was] also a CEC [requirement], and when people respected and implemented the CEC, it was greatly helping PS. In my mind, if we blew off the CEC, we would be giving everyone else permission to blow it off as well," which would mean giving tacit permission to not support PowerShell.

"So, I nixed Lee's design and jammed the .NET workflow on the team and condemned it to the dustbin of history."

"The two problems (in my mind) were that .NET workflow was not factored correctly, so there was a strong coupling between a *task* and the *host*. This meant that there was little to no *task* ecosystem. The idea had been that a *task* written for one host would work with *every* host. It didn't.

"Our implementation was elegant but made it too easy to do the wrong thing, and hard to the right thing [because it was too fine grained]. I don't know what the effects would have been on cmdlet support if we blew off the CEC and gone with Lee's implementation, but I'm absolutely convinced that people would have used it and loved it."

"In the end," Holmes says, "most people that were shaking the bars demanding workflow support realized that they didn't really care about robust, restartable, multi-user dynamic process control systems. They [had just been] looking for scripting all along, [and] PowerShell had handled [that] just fine since 2006."

Data Streams

Jim Truher says, "One of my original thoughts for the shell [was] that we would be able to have flexible and dynamic creation of data streams. Initially, I wanted to have multiple streams for Verbose, Debug, Progress, etc., and these streams could be duplicated and bifurcated so you could have multiple readers of all the different streams. If you need a new stream, no problem, just create and use it. I thought it would make creating a hosting application, and hosting the shell, a much simpler thing and *way* more flexible (I had been inspired by the bash ability to create new file streams via exec). I thought it would be super useful since we already knew we wanted these extra streams, but I wanted to have a way to extend and make it more awesome.

"I may have spec'd it (I don't recall), but I met with the developer to talk about it, and I could not get him to see the point—he couldn't get past the need for three streams (stdin, stdout, stderr). I spent a lot of time trying to get this to happen, but to no avail."

Traditional command-line tools have always had three streams:

- **stdin** is how commands accepted input. That might come from the keyboard, or it might come from another file. It's text, regardless of where it comes from, in keeping with traditional shells' focus on text-based operations.
- **stdout** is where a command sent its output, often for display on-screen, but potentially connected to the stdin of another command. Again, all text.
- **stderr** is where commands wrote errors. Nearly always displayed on-screen, having this as a distinct stream enabled error output to be separated from the command's "intended" output.

PowerShell *does* have more streams than that today. It sets aside different "channels," or "pipelines" for a command's intended output (the "Success" pipeline), and for Verbose, Debug, Warning, Error, and Informational output. But those streams are much simpler things than Truher originally envisioned.

"Right," Snover agrees. "This was the whole point about, 'Power-Shell is actually a multi-branch object-flow system with a command-line interface syntax.'"

"If you recall, we originally intended to write GUIs which would generate richer, directed graphs—including cycles—to support monitoring and distributed monitoring/diagnostic/fix-it flows." The idea was that streams could be split, combined, redirected, and cycled back at each other: have an error? Direct it to a specific process, and then loop back to try again.

But, Snover says, "Then we had a developer which took all that and hardcoded it all away." Rather than coding the engine to support streams *that might not necessarily be running in a purely command-line environment,* the developer presumed a command-line and hardcoded the engine accordingly. By the time the team had figured it out, it was too late and too expensive to go back and change it.

"This is probably my biggest technical regrets about the shell," Truher says.

"Ugh," Snover agrees.

Tainted Data

This, Jeffrey Snover says, is one of his bigger screw-ups.

He had an idea that PowerShell would mark the origins of the data it worked with. Security was, after all, one of the team's top principles and priorities. Untrusted data, or data derived from untrusted data, would be marked as "tainted." You could then set up boundaries where "tainted" data could flow and could not flow.

Unfortunately, the idea came late in the game for v1, but Snover felt that either it got into v1, or it would wind up being a "breaking change" in some future version of PowerShell. So, he says, "I really crossed some lines to get it jammed into v1. It was messy, I was a jerk, and I was totally wrong on this one. [Program Manager] Hilal [Al-Hilali] and Charlie [Chase] were the adults in the room and I was the disruptive child. In the end, Bruce [Payette] and Lee [Holmes] kept finding flaws in the design. I was fine with shipping flaws and fixing them afterwards, but Lee convinced me that this was the wrong approach to take with security."

PowerShell today still has no internal concept for "untrusted" or "tainted" data.

COMMUNITY

The MVPs

Microsoft launched their Most Valuable Professional (MVP) Award program in the mid-1990s, as a way of recognizing members of the general public who devoted their time and skills to helping Microsoft's customers—all on a voluntary basis. Initially, the program focused on professionals who were extremely active in online Q&A forums (originally on the CompuServe service, as the Internet hadn't yet become widespread), as they provided a kind of unofficial, free support channel for Microsoft customers.

Later, Microsoft began recognizing other kinds of "community support" efforts, including book authors and conference speakers, user group leaders, podcasters, open source project contributors, and more. Essentially, if you were volunteering a bunch of your time to help support and uplift your fellow Microsoft users, you were a potential MVP. The award is an annual one, and some notable MVPs have been consecutively awarded for well over a decade.

Although they've been rearranged and reorganized in various ways over the years—they're now part of the "Cloud and Datacenter" MVP specialization—PowerShell has always had MVPs. They've been amongst its biggest fans and loudest enthusiasts, and amongst its most outspoken critics. At events like the annual MVP Summit, they'd meet directly with PowerShell team members to test new features, advocate for changes, report bugs and inefficient patterns, and more. They come from the ranks of software developers, independent software vendors, systems administrators, and much more. They're the ones who introduced much of the general community to PowerShell for the first time, and they're often the ones who supported people in their initial steps and stumbles into The PowerShell World.

It's worth noting that, over time, the MVP program's priorities (and budget) constantly shift. Setting out specifically to "earn your MVP" can be a frustrating, fruitless endeavor, because the program's award criteria are typically opaque, and it's hard to guess what program administrators might be "looking for" in any given award cycle. But setting aside the program and its vagaries, it's worth looking at some of PowerShell's earliest MVPs, for they are very much part of The PowerShell Story.

Meet the MVPs

There have been literally dozens—possibly even hundreds—of "PowerShell MVPs" since the product's 2006 launch. This book highlights the thoughts from some of the earliest and longest-running PowerShell MVPs, including Jeff Hicks, Keith Hill, and Jim Christopher. That selection is more a reflection of a book's finite space, however, than a commentary on the incredible, diverse community of PowerShell MVPs over the years.

Jeff Hicks' scripting career started with VBScript, and he was a frequent contributor to the Q&A forums on ScriptingAnswers.com. When PowerShell launched in 2006, it was an obvious thing for Jeff to flip to, and he co-authored some of the first books ever published about PowerShell v1, including *Windows PowerShell: TFM*. He was first awarded the MVP Award in 2007.

Jim Christopher was a software developer when PowerShell came out, but also handling tasks that would later become known as "DevOps." He was the "Build Master" for his company at the time, responsible for making sure software was properly "built" and packaged for deployment. A lot of automation was involved, and at one point he said, "I wish I could use Perl, because I have a lot of file-munging to do [which Perl is good at], but I promised myself I would never use Perl again." Perl is a bit of a hot mess as a language, and his employer actually was pretty anti-Perl as well. But they *were* a Microsoft shop, and so Microsoft's new shell seemed worth looking at. It turned into a classic PowerShell situation: all hands on deck to do a bunch of manual work, and Jim sails in and gets it all done in a couple of hours in PowerShell.

Keith Hill also worked in software development, and before PowerShell's 2006 release was working for a company that did cross-platform development across Windows and HPUX (a UNIX variant). They had a fairly sizable set of regression tests that had to be performed frequently, and so automation looked attractive.

"Wouldn't it be nice," Hall thought, "if there was some kind of C# shell that we could do this with?" He ran across a job posting that kind of alluded to one, but never heard anything about it afterwards. A bit later, he saw a conference session delivered by Jeffrey Snover and Jim Truher—and there was his "C# shell." Hall got in touch with the team, and wound up being a part of the early Monad betas. Syntax, Hall recalls, was fluid at the time, with the team still deciding between programming language-style operators like ‹ or ›, and shell-style operators like the -lt and -gt PowerShell wound up with.

*Jason Helmick was a trainer at Interface Technical Training in Phoenix, AZ, mainly teaching messaging (Exchange Server) and VBScript. Exchange administrators at the time were really grasping for ways to do automation, and were just being buried in their own workloads. VBScript, as you've learned, was a partial solution, but it came with a high learning curve and a lot of complexity. Helmick downloaded the Monad beta and played with it, but within a couple of hours was thinking, "This can't be true." People just didn't seriously believe that Microsoft would follow-through with a shell like that, and were sure it would be abandoned. Helmick didn't look at any of the Exchange Server 2007 previews, though, and so didn't make the connection that Monad—PowerShell—was being prepped to overhaul Exchange administration. When Exchange Server 2007 shipped, everyone dashed to figure out their migration plans—and ran across PowerShell. It was a "stunning, shocking surprise," Helmick remembers, and at that point he threw himself into it full-speed. He pressed Interface's owner, Mike Lajoya, to let Helmick write one of the first training courses on PowerShell. "We have to do this," Helmick remembers telling him. And they did.

Adopting PowerShell

Hicks remembers a difficult learning curve for Windows administrators first engaging with PowerShell. Many "approached it as some kind of direct replacement for VBScript—just a programming language," he says. Many of PowerShell's earliest and most enthusiastic adopters were *developers,* and so many of the online examples and tutorials administrators would run across looked a lot like C# programs, he recalls. His focus became teaching PowerShell *as a shell* to an administrator-specific audience, a decision that catapulted him into the limelight.

Christopher remembers the world being very binary at the outset. You had people who could, "see it," he says, "and who could see how game-changing this would be, and then another group who didn't understand why they'd ever 'go back.'" Dropping the GUI and moving to a command-line felt, for many at the time, like a failure or regression. And it can be scary: whereas a GUI might bury something dangerous under five "are you sure?" dialog boxes, a command could take the whole system down with one keystroke. "I'd give talks, and I'd have like one slide as an intro, and then I'd throw up the console, and you could see a lot of people in the room just get tense."

Helmick remembers it being "not so much like 'adoption,' because it was slow. Very scary to a lot folks," he says. "I'd show it in all the Exchange classes, all the VBScript classes, but it was definitely slow. Running a class on PowerShell, we could get one to go once a quarter, but it was just a handful of people. It didn't really start to have a noticeable uptick until 2008, when Don Jones started becoming really well-known as a PowerShell guy, and started putting the books out. More people started talking about it, and started to get the idea. Classes could run almost every month from that point. People started asking specifically about PowerShell."

The Role of the MVP Community

Hicks says, "People very much looked at us, the MVPs of the time, and asked, 'so what is this PowerShell thing and how am I supposed to use it?'" Somewhat unusually for a new technology product from Microsoft, PowerShell was a bit under the radar. There were no Microsoft Official Curriculum courses, no certification exams, and little in the way of formal guidance—a reflection on the PowerShell team's small size, small budget, and "skunk works" existence at that point.

Christopher found the PowerShell MVPs to be a diverse group. Nothing was cookie-cutter: you had an Ops person next to an InfoSec person next to a database administrator (DBA), all talking about problems and solutions. That diversity was a huge difference from other technical communities at the time: the group abstracted themselves from *what* they did for a living, and instead talked about *how* they were doing it.

Hall feels that the PowerShell team really solicited and valued feedback from their MVPs. He says it felt good that MVPs represented the target audience really well, helping the team come to better decisions. The team constantly posed new questions to their MVPs, using them as a proxy for what the rest of the world might need or prefer.

Where are We Now?

"I think for the most part, we've got MVPs—in fact, a whole lot more people who aren't MVPs—who are blogging, and writing, and speaking at conferences and user groups, who are talking about PowerShell from an admin perspective," Hicks says. Since 2006, he says, PowerShell's audience has come a long way. There's more of a spectrum, with plenty of resources available for absolute newcomers, and with plenty of resources available all the way up to an incredible level of complexity and expertise.

"The mindset is there now," Christopher says. "People know you really can't get by as whatever your job is, without having this kind of ability. It's almost been like a disruptive technology—it feels very much like you can't live without it. I struggle now to find people who aren't using it, and they are all comfortable with it."

Hall says PowerShell is now something "mature, that I can depend on," especially now that it's gone cross-platform. He's still bummed in that he doesn't think PowerShell has gotten as wide of an adoption as it could: he gets his coworkers to use it over Cmd.exe, but has to show them stuff that's meaningful to them to get them to do it. He's been able to lure them in, but only a few of them actually do any scripting. "There's no reason we should be using Cmd.exe," he says. "It took a lot of convincing to show people that you could run the same command in PowerShell!"

What Does the Community Look Like?

Before PowerShell, and despite the ready availability of Internet forums, administrators never congregated around VBScript. There were few communities for VBScript, Hicks remembers, and much of what was online was Microsoft TechNet Q&A forums. "I don't think there really was community in the way that we have it now," he says. "There were no conferences, and I can't think of a single user group that was VBScript-specific." PowerShell, on the other hand, has been a rallying point: there are PowerShell conferences across the world, PowerShell user groups in dozens of cities, hundreds of PowerShell-specific blogs and websites, and more. PowerShell represents a technology that solves a problem, and something that brings real value to businesses and to individuals' careers. That, in turn, encourages people to get together, share information, and support each other, in a way VBScript never did. "One, PowerShell was easier for people to learn and adopt than VBScript," Hicks points out, "which gets more people using it. And then, they realize all the crazy things they can do, and they're inspired to share."

Helmick has strong memories and feelings about the PowerShell community. He says, "One of the most fascinating things to me is I never felt like I was the geek out on some weird limb doing a weird thing. I thought I saw PowerShell as solving a huge problem, and I didn't understand why the uptick was slow. But when there were more people talking about it—more forums websites, more books, more videos—you started to notice something. A lot of the IT people who were starting to show interest—and this was hard, if you were newer, and all your experience was in a GUI, or you had no programming experience, this was scary—guys started to help each other on these forums, figure out how to do things. Forums at the time would flame you if you asked what they thought was a stupid question, and so people wouldn't go to forums. But the community around PowerShell was all new, and they were all newbies, and so you got a different feel to that community. You asked a question and you got an answer. So you started to get reliable, friendly forums, and that started to solidify community.

"So many people were willing to help each other learn, so they could all just get their jobs done. It was okay to be a fanboy! It was okay to be excited that you could see solutions that didn't exist, that were not possible to achieve some of these by yourself. PowerShell got everyone excited about it and they could see their future solutions and their future career. That community really stuck together. People who never spoke up in a community before (I was one of them) started to speak up and wanted to help out, and talk about it.

"You started to see user groups pop up—that got exciting. Windows people hadn't been excited about something before. Snover helped—he was at every conference, and he was so approachable. You had

Don Jones and Jeff Hicks at conferences, and they were friendly, and you could just talk to them. It made it feel more comfortable and less scary, and everyone in the community never forgot that. We just kept helping each other, and newcomers learned that that was the way to do things, and so it kept going."

Changing MVPs' Careers

If PowerShell had an impact on its audience, then it often had a life-changing impact on its MVPs. Hicks says, "If PowerShell had never been here, I really don't know what I would be doing today. Between the books, video training, speaking at conferences, classroom training—I wouldn't have gotten the equivalent amount of work in VBScript. I'm not sure who I'd even be working for. PowerShell made my career, and made it possible for me to be where I am today, working from home and enjoying my work."

The thing PowerShell really did for Christopher was solidify his internal need to "get things done." He says he's never enjoyed talking about how he did something, necessarily, but he loves accomplishing something and being able to point to that. PowerShell let him "find a place where I could express that," he says, and it's pervaded his attitude toward everything else. Even when working as a consultant, he says, "I would look at the business outcomes they wanted and apply the same principles that working inside PowerShell would have needed, and I could bring that to them."

Hall says PowerShell has been a pretty significant part of his career since 2006. Having MVP status was a game-changer, too: it's something his bosses have touted, and he was one of only one or two MVPs in the company. Being able to contact Microsoft people directly to get answers definitely helped him be rated as a high performer. He's used opportunities to give PowerShell "brown bag" sessions to help other people get ahead. PowerShell's definitely made him more productive. He recalls one time when the company was switching to Microsoft Team Foundation Services for source control. They'd been using an older source control offering, which had recently been sold to a one-man ship and no longer felt like a safe bet. But they had fifteen years of code history in there! Hall wrote a PowerShell script that checked out every check-in from the old system, including commit messages, and checked them all into TFS, preserving all that history. "That's just one example," he says, "of the tasks it's let me do."

PowerShell's impact on Helmick's career was extreme. "It's funny, I've been threatening to open up a hot dog stand for 15-20 years. Not a joke! The last time I threatened to do that was before Monad came out. I don't have a hot dog stand, and I don't miss it. PowerShell totally changed my career. As a teacher, I could help people with something I was passionate about and I believed in. It was a technical solution for me as a consultant and as an engineer. My career as a teacher in one city wasn't enough any more—I wanted to reach more people, especially ones who were also helping other people. That led me to help co-found PowerShell.org, and I helped establish PowerShell Summit. It all eventually led to me becoming a Program Manager on the PowerShell team at Microsoft, which is my dream job. PowerShell is directly responsible for me having my dream job, helping take PowerShell into the future."

Shout-Outs

Many of the original PowerShell MVPs have since fallen off the global radar, moving on to other interests and career opportunities. But the ones that are still "in" PowerShell have strong memories, and respect, for those peers. "I think early on, people like Mow [Marc van Orsouw] had an impact on people. Richard Siddaway, certainly, had an impact on people. Those are two that immediately come to mind," Hicks says.

"It'd be easier to point out MVPs that haven't influenced me,"

Christopher says, but he offered special thanks to Oisín Grehan (@oising on Twitter), for "being a developer, being curious, and being a good person—someone I want to be around." Adam Driscoll (@adamdriscoll), who "has the job I want, and he does the things I want to do, and I kind of hate him a little bit for it, in a loving kind of way. For being a developer and just letting the boundaries go." Doug Finke (@dfinke): "I really admire [him], not just on a professional level, but he's just super interesting." PowerShell team member Lee Holmes: "Not an MVP," Christopher admits, "but the kind of guy you look at and think, 'I want to be like you when I grow up.'" And finally, Christopher really admires Chrissy LeMaire (@cl): "Just watching what she's doing and rallying a community around, I love it, and I never figured out how to be able to do that myself."

Some of Helmick's influencers are less well-known: Toni Allardice, who really convinced me to start the user group that I wouldn't shut up about wanting to start. That was a big thing. Mike Lajoya at ITT who supported me in creating that PowerShell course, and giving me the room to do that. But the primary guiding figures for me have always been Jeffrey Snover (@jsnover on Twitter)— the way the man thinks he pretty incredible. Between the way he communicates, and the people who come around him, he's just amazing. Don Jones (@concentrateddon) has been a primary impact on me in this entire journey, and on the entire community for a very long time. He's number one on my list. Jeff Hicks (@jeffhicks) and Richard Siddaway—we became kind of the four musketeers with Don. Oh, and don't let me forget Mike Pfeiffer (@mike_pfeiffer), who helped me start that user group and has been my compatriot through much of this."

The MVP-Microsoft Relationship

Different product teams have different relationships with "their" MVPs. Some maintain a respectful distance; others, like the PowerShell team, embrace their super-fans (who are often also their super-critics). A memorable example comes from the lead-up to PowerShell v3.0, which happened under Microsoft Vice President Steven Sinofsky. Sinofsky had come in on the heels of the disastrous Windows Vista release, and he felt that one of Microsoft's "sins" was being "overly transparent" with customers about what the company was working on. Talking about in-development features, he felt, set up unreasonable expectations, so that no matter what eventually shipped would always feel disappointing. Sinofsky preferred "translucency," he said, opting for a more carefully curated narrative to share with customers.

But PowerShell v3 was planning to debut a major new feature, and a new milestone from the original Manifesto. They needed feedback, and they needed it to come from their bigger fans—and critics. So the team "put their employee badges on the line," making a firm case that the MVPs could be trusted to respect the trust that Microsoft showed them. As a result, after an annual MVP Summit event in Redmond, a group of PowerShell MVPs were quietly led to a room full of computers, and allowed some time to experiment with v3's new "Workflow" feature. Their feedback was recorded—on camera!—and much of it was incorporated into the end product. For example, the fact that PowerShell workflows start with the keyword `Workflow`, and not `Function`, came from that meeting.

That's one example, and over the years there have been many more. With today's more open, open-source, community-engaged Microsoft, that story can seem like a bit of a "so what?" event, but at the time, it was a major Happening. It was also evidence of how closely the PowerShell team in particular engaged their community, and the lengths they were willing to go to to maintain that engagement.

My PowerShell Story

While I've tried to write this book in the third-person voice that is traditional for histories like this, this chapter is about me, and so I'll briefly switch to first-person. I hope you don't mind the indulgence.

I had been a freelancer since being laid off at Christmas 2000, and by 2003 had written a number of books. One, *Windows Server 2003 Delta Guide*, had earned me my first Microsoft MVP Award. Another, *Managing Windows with VBScript and WMI*, was published in 2004 and put me firmly on the map as someone dedicated to Windows administrative automation. VBScript was, as you know by now, all we had to work with back then, but by late 2004 and into 2005, Microsoft had started releasing previews of "Monad," which at the time was expected to be called "Microsoft Shell." I ran a website called ScriptingAnswers.com at the time, which mainly consisted of VBScript Q&A forums. I quickly added a Monad forum, because it seemed like this new shell might be the future for administrative automation.

By late 2005, I was working for SAPIEN Technologies, whose main product was a script editing tool called PrimalScript. SAPIEN's leaders agreed that this "Monad thing" was likely to be a big deal, and started making the changes needed to let PrimalScript support the new shell and its new language. I also started writing *Windows PowerShell: TFM*, which we planned to publish under a new "SAPIEN Press" brand. It would wind up being the first-ever print book on PowerShell.

In late 2006, Microsoft had decided that TechEd Europe 2006, to be held in November in Barcelona, Spain, would be the place where Monad—now officially named PowerShell—would be unleashed on the world. Jeffrey Snover was eager to show that PowerShell already had a supportive and active ecosystem, and so he invited SAPIEN to send someone to present with him on-stage. That was a huge marketing opportunity for the company, of course, and so I was dispatched to Spain.

My understanding is that we'd present on Tuesday, so I arrived Sunday with plans to depart Wednesday. When I arrived, I managed to Skype Jeffrey Snover, and confirmed where we'd meet. "We've been moved to Thursday," he said, "but you're here all week, right?" I stammered, "uh, sure," and immediately called American Express. I needed my flights changed, my hotel extended (and I didn't speak much Spanish), and I needed to buy some clothes. I also sent a direct message to SAPIEN's Alex Riedel, who—time zones notwithstanding—I knew would be awake. "This is going to be a pricey change," I warned him. "What's this worth to you?" "I don't know," he replied, "probably ten grand or so." Well, it wasn't that much, so I put American Express to work. The presentation went off without a hitch, and for a long time, PrimalScript was the premier editing environment for PowerShell.

The next year, I got another call from Snover. "I'm scheduled to present on PowerShell at TechEd 2007 in New Orleans," he said, "but I'm scheduled to do something else. You want to do the talk for me?" Giggling inside, I said yes: I'd spoken at conferences several times a year since 1998, but never at a major event like TechEd. This felt like a huge break.

Prior to the event, I got a call from the organizers: "we let people pre-register for sessions," they said, "and your PowerShell one is full. Can we schedule a repeat?" An emphatic yes from me! A few weeks later: "It's full again. We're going to live-stream it as well, is that okay?" Giggle. Yes!

So I show up for this session, my talk more precisely planned and timed than any I'd ever given. There's a bank of spotlights aimed at the stage, making it incredibly hot. There's a broadcast-style camera in front of me, to my left, and to my right. The audio guy puts *two* microphone packs on me, just in case one fails mid-session. "Okay," the coordinator says, "we have your slides loaded on our computer and you need to present those from there because that's what's hooked up to LiveMeeting but when you are ready to do a demo you can use your laptop just make sure you are really clear you're about to do a demo because we have to start the screen sharing in the back and it takes a few seconds to start got all that anything else you need okay here we go."

Just like that. No commas, just one long run-on blast of information.

So now I'm sweating my ass off, I've got Logistics Hell unfolding in front of me, cameras ready to capture every gaffe, and in strolls Jeffrey Snover. "Uh," I stammer, "why are you here?"

"Oh," he says, plopping down front and center next to my partner, Christopher. "PowerShell is getting a TechEd award, so they rescheduled me to be here, but I still wanted you to do the talk. Break a leg!"

House lights down. Spotlights *up*, somehow, making it even hotter. I start.

My presentation style, if you've never seen me speak, uses a good bit of snark. "You can either learn PowerShell," I said, "or you can learn to say, 'would you like fries with that?'" was one way I tried to communicate how important PowerShell was, and it's a phrase that lingers in the community to this day. Big laffs! But in my lower vision, I see Snover lean over to Christopher and whisper something. My sweat output increases. I'd *just* had my MVP moved over to the PowerShell team and I didn't need this guy pissed at me! But I kept going: I'd really scripted this session out and I didn't have room to deviate. Throughout, the crowd all laughed at he right spots, the demos went off without a hitch—LiveMeeting logistics notwithstanding—and Snover and Christopher kept whispering into each others' ears like a couple of schoolchildren.

Session ends. Spotlights down, a bit. House lights up. Snover stands, says, "good session," and walks out. I take a few questions from the audience, literally shaking like a leaf in a hurricane. Sweat is pouring down my back so hard, I'm surprised I didn't short out the mic packs, and I know I grossed out the tech who removed them. I weakly stumble off the stage, and Christopher comes over.

"What," I whispered fiercely, "were you two talking about?"

"Oh," Christopher says, "when you made the fries remark, he said he was glad you were up there, because that needed saying and he wouldn't have been able to say it."

Oh. Okay. "What about the rest?"

"We realized it was making you nervous so we just kept doing it. He really liked the session."

"I need a drink."

Snover and I developed quite a rapport over the years. We did two or three "PowerShell Unplugged" sessions, which are absolutely worth looking up online if you get a minute. I don't know how educational they were for people, but they were entertaining as hell for everyone, including us. At the last one I did, at Microsoft Ignite 2015[10], Jeffrey pulled one last one on me. He showed that First Follower - Lessons in Leadership from the Dancing Guy[11] video before the session started (there were copyright concerns about showing it during the session, which was being recorded). Afterwards, he officially named me PowerShell's First Follower. "I'm the crazy shirtless guy," Jeffrey said, referring to the video, "and Don's the one who showed everyone else how to dance." Then we started the session, while I was still *nearly* teared-up.

PowerShell meant a *lot* to me over much of my career, and even past the point where I moved into leadership and had to turn away from the technology on a daily basis. I have a screen-shot showing my session, "A Practical Overview of DSC," as the number one session at TechEd, and "Windows PowerShell Practices and Patterns" as number six. I was listed as the second-most effective presenter that same year. Huge career milestones for someone who, at the time, made a lot of my income from conferences and the follow-on work they led to. But all things that never would have happened, never *could* have happened, if it hadn't been for PowerShell. Even to this day, my involvement in The PowerShell community—from writing books to helping found PowerShell.org and PowerShell Summit— has given me more lifelong friends and colleagues than anything else I've done, or could have imagined doing.

When Snover was fighting to keep Monad alive and to find it a place to live, I'm not sure he had, "vibrant, supportive, friendly global community" in mind. Or maybe he did—he's a bright guy that way. Regardless, he got it, or rather we *all* got it. In fact, it's arguable that despite PowerShell's massive positive *technological* impact, it's *real*

---

[10]https://bit.ly/MSIgnitePSU15
[11]https://bit.ly/FirstFollower

impact was in how it brought together an audience that had never had much reason to come together before. A friendly, supportive, professional community of people who saw PowerShell's potential for themselves, their careers, and their lives.

Their story is the best one.

Impact

There's no question that PowerShell had a variety of impacts on the world. Inside Microsoft, PowerShell eventually became a requirement of Windows' Common Engineering Criteria, or CEC, mandating that Windows components provide some means of administration via PowerShell—either by exposing .NET classes, by providing PowerShell cmdlets, by instrumenting in Windows Management Instrumentation, or something else. Products outside

Windows—starting with Exchange, of course, but moving into SharePoint Server, SQL Server, and other major server products—gradually jumped on board. Eventually, PowerShell became standard operating procedure for at least some degree of administrative automation.

Third parties were impacted, too: companies like VMware, Amazon Web Services, Citrix, Quest Software, and many more adopted PowerShell as a common administrative layer, to the delight of Microsoft-centric administrators everywhere.

And it's those administrators where PowerShell may have had the most impact. Admins like Jayson Bennett:

> Just previous to getting very interested in PowerShell, I had just started working at a children's hospital as an Active Directory and general systems administrator. My first project was to go through all of the user accounts and determine which ones had not logged in for 30 days and disable them all. At that time there were 20,000 users in the AD environment, and I really didn't want to go through them all by hand.
>
> In doing a bit of research, I found out about all of the cool things that PowerShell could do when it came to AD. I signed up for Jason Helmick's class based on *Learn Windows PowerShell in a Month of Lunches,* and dove in headfirst. I returned from his class and was able to come up with a script that went through every active user to check the last logon date and disable everyone that had not logged in for 30 days. Without PowerShell, that project would have taken me weeks to complete.
>
> As far as I know, that script is still running weekly on a scheduled task nine years after I wrote it.

Didn't want to do it by hand comes up a lot when you speak to PowerShell enthusiasts: while smaller businesses may have been content to throw manual labor at their administrative problems, most actual admins felt the same way that big enterprises did: manual effort *sucked*. Nobody wanted to do the same thing all day, every day, and PowerShell provided a way out. Chris Thomas agrees:

> I started learning PowerShell around 2012 or so, but never found a real good use for it with my day-to-day job at the time. It wasn't until my school district decided we'd buy $1.4 million worth of iPads, well before Apple had any sort of tools to help that work at scale, that I saw real value in PowerShell for myself. The Apple ID creation and verification process was very manual. I asked for time to sit down and write a script to try and do it for us and was allowed to. It took my longer than I care to admit, but I cobbled together a script that would reach into the generic Apple ID exchange mailboxes we had setup, look for the most recent email from apple, use the verification link to browse to the website, tab around (because I didn't know how to work with webpage elements at the time) and fill in the appropriate stuff and then verify the Apple ID. We ended up letting it run for a weekend and it did a couple thousand Apple ID's with very little interaction or errors. I was pretty proud of it.
>
> I've been in K12 IT since 2000 and I was always the type of tech that would memorize the number of tabs, arrows and enters to proceed through the Next-Next-Finish type installers when I'd have to install it on a lab of 30. This was before I had an automation mindset. A little later in my career I had my 'batch cheat sheet' with commands I had learned and I'd write batch files so I could login to computers and just 'run -> x:\a.bat' and made life easier. Later I discovered psexec and was thrilled to not have to leave my seat to accomplish tasks

around the school district. I still struggled with HOW to execute some things on remote machines though. Once I saw PowerShell though I fell in love because the syntax was so easy to understand with some practice.

At this point in my career, I don't even care what the technology is ... VMware, SharePoint, Google, RESTful API ... if I can work with a SME on that topic I can help them write PowerShell to make their lives easier. It's an amazing tool!

That's another common theme: *with PowerShell, I think I got this.* Administrators—even those coming to PowerShell years after its launch—feel *enabled.* But sometimes the impact is more personal. Take Josh Duffney's blog post[12], and one of my favorite bits from it:

I've seen tweets ... before and have even heard compelling stories about how a sys admin learned Power-Shell and then got a 10% raise. Hearing stuff like this is always motivating to me, but it's not only motivating, it's now a *reality* for me. I received an offer that has doubled my salary!

Stories abound of administrators who hunkered down, learned PowerShell—often on their own, with little or no support from their employer—and then moved on to a job paying 10% more, 50% more, 200% more, or even 300% more. While not every employer recognizes the financial value of administrative automation, *many do,* and they're always hunting for qualified people. Those companies tend to recognize that paying more for a solid automation person more than pays itself off, so they're happy to do it.

Take Brian's story:

---

[12]https://bit.ly/DuffneyDouble

2002 – 2005: Doing a mix of help desk, Windows, Netware, and Linux administration at an arts organization, doing everything from install printer drivers, to writing Perl scripts to automate tasks on our Linux servers.

2005 – 2015ish: Move to a large university to become their Exchange admin. When 2007 rolls around, I'm pleasantly surprised at how much I enjoy using PowerShell and the ease of administration that comes with it. I become known as a 'PowerShell guy' and script writing becomes a regular part of my job. The limited scope of the job starts to wear on me until...

2016-Present: the university kicks off the Office 365 migration project. I'm no longer the Exchange admin. Now, I straddle the line between admin and dev. I level up my skills and treat writing code with a seriousness I hadn't employed before. Writing modules, unit testing, creating in-house standards, and setting up a dev pipeline for the Windows team occupy large portions of my time. I contributed code to the migration project as well as replacing legacy code for onboarding, license management, and many, many more. Then I begin training coworkers, helping them move away from the 'clicky-click' module of administration.

Don Jones's books, the PowerShell Summit, and a large community of Powershell users that share their knowledge had a huge impact on my career. From financial, personal/career growth, to job satisfaction, PowerShell has had a huge, beneficial impact on my life.

That highlights how for many Microsoft-centric administrators, PowerShell was their first experience with real *community*. A group of people who share their knowledge pretty selflessly, take time to answer questions in online forums, and just generally help each other out. It's incredibly empowering, and it's the kind of thing that helps you differentiate between your *career* and your current *job*. That community is there for your *career*.

In Alexander Holmeset's post, "My story on how I got into automation and why you should do the same,"[13] he tells about how his PowerShell journey moved him into IT, and eventually into a senior consulting position. He writes:

> By starting to learn PowerShell you make yourself more valuable and indispensable to your employer. It's even easier to apply to new jobs, as you can see a lot of job ads these days that have PowerShell as a requirement. Even if you are an IT veteran and never done any automation at all, you should start thinking about learning Power-Shell. Why waste time on huge repetitive tasks, when you can get more done by automating?

Like many other admins, Steven Judd shared his PowerShell story in a blog post,[14] hoping to inform and inspire others—a goal that's become commonplace in The PowerShell community. He writes:

> I started looking at Monad around Beta 2 and subsequent pre-release versions including the official release. Frankly, I didn't understand it. I was an administrator not a developer and the concepts of objects and APIs did not resonate with me. In 2008 I took a PowerShell class taught by a Microsoft employee and thought it was OK, but wasn't sure it was going to replace my entrenched knowledge and library of VBScript based scripts.

A very common feeling, in PowerShell's first half-decade. Like many administrative tools, its value wasn't always obvious at first glance. But after a while:

---

[13]https://bit.ly/HolmesetAutomation
[14]https://bit.ly/JuddPSJourney

Since I had been using VBScript and batch files for quite a while, I was still trying to get used to working in PowerShell. I had VBScript examples for handling repetitive actions. One of these actions was sending an email from a script. Since I was converting my work to PowerShell, I needed a way to send email from PowerShell. That's when I found the Send-MailMessage cmdlet. "You mean I only need one command to send email? I don't need multiple lines of code like VB-Script?" That alone convinced me that PowerShell was a game changer for how I will get work done going forward.

Steven then gets into the gritty reality of life in the world of corporate IT:

Let me explain how this played out for me personally. I work in the energy sector. Times were great when prices were high, up until 2015. Then when prices came crashing down, times were not great. We have had layoffs at our company every year starting in 2015 through 2019, excepting 2017. Not minor cuts either. The smallest cut was 2019 at 10%. The largest was 33%. That is a lot of people exiting the organization in a short amount of time.

It is my belief that my willingness to learn, share, and automate that has kept me from being laid off. There always are other factors in play, but I think being able to demonstrate a tangible return, as well as lifting others up was the difference maker. All of us that are involved in automation are able to "do more with less," a common phrase uttered by business people everywhere.

Do more with less. That's PowerShell's mantra, and it does indeed line up precisely with what businesses always seem to be asking for.

Those stories come from across the globe, like this one from Thomas Maurer in Switzerland:

> I think one of my biggest challenges but also one of the best learning experiences, and the project which gave me a jumpstart in my career, was when we were starting to build a SharePoint Hosting environment based on SharePoint 2010. It was in 2009 when I started working to develop my own PowerShell modules, working with web services, and much more. PowerShell still was missing a couple of important features, and we worked around this using C# code. I started to share my learning about PowerShell on my blog (www.thomasmaurer.ch), which helped me to get exposure in the Microsoft community. And until today, I have a couple of blog posts from 2009, which people are still looking up fairly regularly. In addition, this project also helped me to get a new job when I showed this project to a Microsoft employee who then recommended me to a successful Microsoft consulting company in Switzerland.
>
> Today I am working for Microsoft, and I am still using PowerShell almost daily, and I am still trying to help the community to get better.

The "this drove my career" theme is increasingly common, and it's especially moving when you look at it over the long term. Carl Davis did:

> While working for a large AntiVirus company in 2007 (starts with an S and ends with C), they asked me to lead the newly formed VMware team. It consisted of three people and I was the only US based associate. I

had always used the command line to get work done in Windows and SQL using DOS or VBScript (if I absolutely had to). Now I had a need to do the same automation in VMware. After a little research I discovered the VIClient created by VMware which was based on PowerShell and I was hooked. I was able to automate almost 100% of my job! I never took a class to learn PowerShell, but learned as I went. I went back into a Windows SysAdmin role and it was amazingly easy to port all the knowledge I gained from VMware over to a Microsoft environment. Now I am attempting to do the same thing with a networking team automating Cisco Infrastructure. My knowledge of PowerShell and Automation has been the sole driver for my career growth over the last 13 years.

Finally, Aaron sums up how so many PowerShell professionals feel:

PowerShell changed my life. I realize that such a statement may seem exaggerated, but every PowerShell enthusiast can relate in some way to the overwhelming benefits, and career opportunities that learning PowerShell has given them.

Changed my life isn't something you hear attached to very many "back-end" technologies like PowerShell. Again, it's hard to say if Jeffrey Snover and his team imagined this kind of impact when they were just setting out, but it's safe to say their efforts are deeply appreciated.

PowerShell Program Manager Jim Truher, who helped ship v1.0, said it best: PowerShell's success wasn't because the team built a shell. Anyone could have built a shell, or just ported one from Unix, as the original Kermit project aimed to do. What the team built was a means for *other people* to more effectively and efficiently build the tools *they* needed. By making PowerShell a "facade" on top of things like .NET, WMI, COM, and more, PowerShell *enabled* its users and creators to work however they felt most comfortable, and still produce something consistent and reusable. *That* was PowerShell's impact.

If PowerShell impacted its community, then the community impacted PowerShell right back. Kenneth Hansen recalls that PowerShell v1 shipped with 84 "contributions" from non-Microsoft individuals—a first for any Microsoft product. That's because, during the Monad beta period, an enormous number of people were downloading and trying the new shell (spurred by ample cheerleading from the team, particularly Jeffrey Snover). Many of them sent in bug reports, suggested changes, or filed other types of issues, resulting in those 84 "outsider" changes.

That pattern would continue through PowerShell's life. Now an open-source project, anyone on GitHub can easily see who's been contributing what to the code base. But even prior to that, the team would often ship a "read me" file with each successive version of PowerShell, quietly giving credit to the fixes, few features, and changed behaviors that had been suggested by PowerShell's passionate fans.

Oh, and they *are* passionate. Kenneth Hansen remembers attending a TechEd Berlin with Jeffrey Snover and some other team members. In addition to a 1,000-person introductory session on PowerShell, the team also held a one-hour general Q&A session. They were desperate to connect with more PowerShell users, understand their experience with the product, and adjust their future plans accordingly. The conference organizers, not fully understanding who and what they were dealing with, scheduled the session for a room that sat just 100 people.

The room packed to fire code capacity, with people looming in the hallway trying to catch a glimpse of the proceedings.

The organizers scheduled a repeat—at 8:30am on the last day of the conference, traditionally a "punishment" time slot for topics that aren't expected to be popular. Once again, the room was packed.

Hansen remembers conferring with Jeffrey after they left the session, and in the span of half an hour, they'd concocted a scheme. They knew Microsoft suffered from a short corporate attention span, which means holding PowerShell sessions at the company's flagship events would always be a battle with whatever the latest new-and-shiny Marketing direction was. So they resolved to somehow bootstrap a "Deep Dive" conference dedicated to PowerShell and run by the community—who could keep it going even if Microsoft's attention waned. The result was the first 50-person "PowerShell Deep Dive," held as part of NetPro's The Experts Conference. That ran for two years before NetPro was purchased by Quest Software, who discontinued the event. But the community, having gotten a taste of an information-dense, intimate, community-led event, wouldn't let go: the next year, a new organization was formed by community members Don Jones, Jason Helmick, Jeff Hicks, and Richard Siddaway, and they held the first PowerShell Summit in Redmond, Washington. That organization, now called The DevOps Collective, Inc., continues to run what is now called PowerShell + DevOps Global Summit annually, along with other automation and DevOps-related events, "PowerShell Saturday" regional events, and more.

CONCLUSION

So there you have it: the history of PowerShell, much of it previously untold.

This book was always meant to bring these stories to light, and to preserve them. PowerShell has made an outsized and, for some, unexpected impact on the IT industry. Not just in the Microsoft world, either: Mac and Linux folks have begun to embrace PowerShell as the right tool for certain jobs, too.

PowerShell's history, like that of many technology products, was a bit chaotic. It was fraught at times, and the fingerprints of its origins remain with it today. Understanding where it comes from is part of the fun.

This book really focused on PowerShell's history through v2.0, prior to the v3 launch. Not that there isn't a lot of story there: v3 saw the launch of PowerShell's Workflow feature (a fairly rousing fail, for the most part) and massively increased cmdlet coverage; v4 saw the launch of Desired State Configuration (which was much more successful that Workflow). From v6 on, *Windows PowerShell* became just *PowerShell,* as it moved to an open-source software model and became available on operating systems besides Windows (something that would have been impossible under Steve Ballmer in the v1 days). Today, *anyone* can become a part of PowerShell's "future history." Dozens of people have committed hundreds, if not thousands, of meaningful improvements and changes to the shell via its GitHub repository[15]. The story of PowerShell gets harder to

---
[15]https://github.com/powershell/powershell

track from that point, as it becomes the story of an entire, global community of people.

There's something worth noting, which is that Windows Power-Shell v2 pretty much established the beating heart of what PowerShell is. If you learned the core PowerShell syntax and "ways of doing things" under v2.0, pretty much nothing has changed for you in all that time. Sure, you've gotten *more* to work with, and things like performance have likely improved, but the language and operational model was pretty much set down in v1 and v2 and remains stable to this day. Talk about protecting your learning investment!

And PowerShell will have a strong future. It's earned its place as the "right tool" for an increasing number of jobs, and it's one of the few technologies in the world to have bootstrapped its own global, tight-knit community. If you're working with PowerShell today, you probably already know how much company you have.

Just don't forget that it was all *almost* started by a hermit crab named Kermit.

Acknowledgements

Obviously, this book couldn't have happened without all the cooperation and input from the early-days PowerShell team members, all of whom were incredibly generous with their time, their anecdotes, and their memories. Jeffrey Snover in particular, of course, but also Jim Truher (who never met a document that wasn't worth keeping), Kenneth Hansen, Lee Holmes, Bruce Payette, Daryl Wray, Charlie Chase, and everyone else who took time for interviews and endless emails. Thanks also to current team member Jason Helmick for help tracking folks down, and for beta-reading.

Big thanks to Simon Goodway for the chapter illustrations, and to Alyssa Morris for her copyediting services (although any remaining ~~erorrs~~ errors are all mine!)

And finally, a huge thanks to everyone in the PowerShell community who've made the first 14 years of PowerShell a wonderful, friendly, supportive, and positive experience for me. To everyone who's walked up at a conference and said hi, know that I really appreciate it. To those who haven't, I hope I'll run into you soon.

APPENDICES

"PowerShell Makes Us All Better at Our Games"

During the time when PowerShell was being created, Microsoft pressed its people *hard* to create innovative new intellectual property (IP), and to then protect that IP by filing patents. For large software companies, their patent portfolio is sometimes more important—and more valuable—than their actual products. And thanks to "patent trolls," companies are strongly incentivized to ensure their own products are "free and clear" of patent conflict, and one of the best ways to do that is to have your own patents.

The PowerShell team was no exception, and they filed for numerous patents related to the new shell. Patents often list multiple inventors, and for many professionals, it's a critical part of their job—as well as a pretty cool recognition—to be listed as an inventor on a patent. Jeffrey Snover recalls:

> I've always taken the position that it is very hard to trace the origin of an idea in a collaborative environment. That is why when it came to patents, my policy was that someone would write it up, send it around for review and then anyone that felt that they had a "significant and meaningful contribution" could add themselves as inventors with no questions asked. We filed a [lot] of patents (more than 40 or 50) and this [process] worked out great.
>
> Mostly.
>
> At some point, I felt that a particular individual was abusing this policy and declaring themselves to be an inventor of things that they really shouldn't have. If

that happened today—I would just go have the difficult conversation with the person but as I said, PowerShell was going to provide us a set of lessons that would make us all better at our game.

I was sufficiently annoyed by this that I decided that the next time I had a patentable idea, I was going use a different process. I was going to limit collaboration and publish it with a just those inventors. I remember having [a] deep insight and the lightbulb went off. I fleshed out the idea enough to bring in a collaborator. I chose Jeff Jones, one of our super smart junior programmers to help me refine the idea and in the process, add enough IP to be one of the inventors. I invited him into my office, explained the new model, discussed the new idea. I forget how it went but at the end of the meeting, he said something to the effect of "Yup – this is a great idea. That is why I came up with it last year. Remember the email I sent you?" I was 100.0% convinced he was wrong. I was metaphysically certain that I had invented that idea just yesterday. Two days before, there was nothing, and now there was a great idea. 10 minutes later, Jeff forwarded the email he had sent me over a year earlier with this very idea. Wow was that a humbling experience.

It was one of the most profound lessons of my life actually. Anyway—I went back to the original model and have been very suspicious of my thinking/perceptions ever since.

"PowerShell," Snover says, "made us all better at our games." The process of bringing such a thing to life definitely changes perspectives and gives you valuable new experiences.

"We Can Leapfrog Linux!"

PowerShell—Monad, at the time—wasn't always a clear-cut win inside Microsoft in the early days. A lot of people needed to understand the competitive landscape, and how PowerShell would approach it, in order to understand the full value proposition. What follows are slides from a deck that Jeffrey Snover used to help position Monad internally. Additional context is included for those less intimately familiar with the subject and some of the specific terms and concepts presented.

If it *seems* like there's a huge focus on Linux here—well, there is. Keep in mind that a real business driver for Microsoft was competing with Linux, which was perceived as having much more powerful administrative automation than Windows.

These slides were provided by Jeffrey Snover and are included with his permission. Some slides from the original deck have been omitted in the interests of space and clarity. The commentary below each slide is the work of this book's author, not Mr. Snover.

Monad – Leapfrogging Linux With Next Generation Automation

Jeffrey Snover
Architect
Windows Server

FOR MORE INFO...   http://Monad

4/21/2020   1

Microsoft projects often had a "home page" on Microsoft's intranet;
the "http://Monad" URL would have pointed to one. Hey, this was
before everyone encrypted everything; forgive the lack of "https:"!

Context

- System management is a <u>critical</u> problem for MSFT
- Major source of dissatisfaction
- Operational and opportunity costs overwhelm our cost benefit
- Admin/Server ratio stinks
- We consistently misunderstand Admins
    - Allchin's Mom and Dave Cutler
- Linux is kicking our butt

2

A concise and unabashed statement of the situation: Linux is kicking our butts!

Monad

- Born out of a Convergence of Insights
- UNIX composable management SUCKS
- Economics matter
- .Net Reflection is the next SQL
- We can Leapfrog Linux

3

Here's the pitch: text-based shells are common and popular, but that's only because people haven't imagined something better. Monad can *be* something better. Note the strong focus on Monad as a competitive advantage for Windows as an operating system; it's an approach you'd likely not see from today's Microsoft, which released their own Linux distribution even as they continue to evolve Windows.

UNIX Composable Management

- A | B | C
  - The heart of Unix composable management
- Means that A didn't do what you wanted to do
  - WHY?
- A is a tight coupling of
  - Get Objects => Process Objects => Output as text
  - "| B | C" uses prayer-based parsing to recreate the object so you can do one of the steps differently
- .NET allows us to do better
  - Pipeline structured objects instead of text
  - Pipeline should be between get/process/Output
- UNIX: Great model – horrible implementation

4

This illustrates Snover's primary argument against text-based shells: the "pipeline" approach *works,* but it was never *designed.* Everything's a hack, and scripts become very convoluted and delicate.

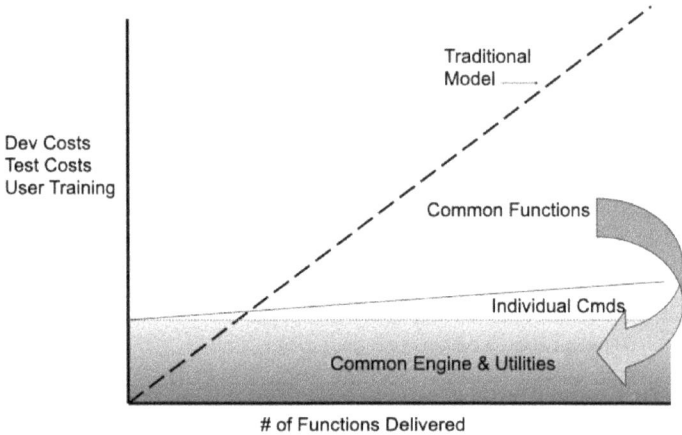

Economics for Developers

This slide conveys the fact that traditional command development doesn't leverage a lot of re-use or synergy. If a developer needs X effort to develop a command, then need $40X$ effort to develop 40 commands. A lot of common functions are written, but they're not centralized into a common engine where every command can leverage them.

.Net Reflection is the Next SQL

- UNIX:
  - Standardized data encoding (ASCII files) allows the emergence of a set of domain-neutral utilities for composition and manipulation (e.g. sed, awk, grep)
- SQL:
  - Standardized data forms (Tables) allow the emergence of a set of domain-neutral utilities for composition and manipulation (e.g. join, query, groupby)
- .NET Reflection:
  - Standardized object forms (.net objects) allow the emergence of a set of domain-neutral utitilities for composition and manipulation (MONAD)

7

This slide is all about data-sharing models. Unix does it through simple text, which is unstructured and fragile. SQL-based databases use structured data in tables. Monad would use .NET Framework's structured objects.

Monad Leapfrogs Linux

- As **powerful** and **composable** as UNIX ksh, Perl, and Ruby
- As **consistent** and **production-oriented** as VMS and AS400
- As **embeddable** as TCL

Make Windows admins the most productive in the industry

8

This is the pitch: Monad can be everything Linux does well, and improve on everything Linux does poorly. It can be more consistent, and more production-oriented. Monad can be *designed* for administration, and be better for that focus.

Big 5 Monad Concepts

1. Commands
   - Classes exposed as CommandLine, API, WS
   - Keep them tiny and leverage MSH to do as much as possible
   - MSH provides parsing, predicate evaluation, data validation, globing, data manipulation
2. Command Family Providers (e.g. navigation)
   - Classes to implement specific sets of functions/Monad provides the Commands
   - Higher levels of semantic/syntactic consistency
3. PropertySets
   - Metadata to give sets of properties standard names
   - Admin friendly abstractions to interact with anything/everything
4. Brokered Methods
   - Methods which provide additional properties or methods to another TYPE
   - Transparent integration of multiple data sources
5. Shared Semantics
   - Set of classes you should use as properties in your classes to facilitate composition and semantic coupling
   - Shifting management from an IS-A to a HAS-A model

9

This slide lays out some of the early key concepts for Monad. Cmdlets and Providers are present. PropertySets, which do exist in PowerShell today but are essentially unknown and unused, are also here. Note that the Extensible Type System is referred to implicitly, with the idea of standardizing property names and making admin-friendly abstractions.

Hello World

```
using System.Management.Automation;
namespace MyNamespace
{
    [CommandDeclaration("myhello", "myworld")]
    public class MyCmdlet : Command
    {
        public override void Begin()
        {
            WriteObject( "myhello/myworld: Begin" );
        }
        public override void Execute()
        {
            WriteObject( "myhello/myworld: Execute called: "
            + CurrentObject.ToString());
        }
        public override void Complete()
        {
            WriteObject( "myhello/myworld: Complete" );
        }
    }//MyCmdlet
}//MyNamespace
```

10

The inevitable "Hello World" example, showing the basic structure of a PowerShell cmdlet written in C#. Cmdlets don't look *exactly* like this because the model evolved significantly during development and usability testing, but this is spiritually very similar to what exists today.

Using Parameters

```
[CommandDeclaration("set", "alias")]
public class SetAliasCommand : AliasCommand
{
    [ParsingMandatoryParameter]
    [ParsingPromptString("Alias Name")]
    [ParsingAllowPipeLineInput]
    [ValidationPattern("[!_a-zA-Z./\\\\][:!_a-zA-Z0-9./\\\\]*")]
    [ParsingParameterMapping(0)]
    public string Name;

    [ParsingMandatoryParameter]
    [ParsingPromptString("Substitution string")]
    [ParsingAllowPipeLineInput]
    [ParsingParameterMapping(1)]
    public string Value;
    public override void Execute()
    {
        aliasTable[Name] = Value;
    }
}
```

```
$ set/alias –name cd –val set/location
$ set/alias cd set/location

$ set/alias
>Alias Name: cd
>Substitution string: set/location

$ ......| set/alias

$ get/alias | set/alias –value XXX
```

11

An example of how a C# developer would define a cmdlet's parameters. Note the support for aliases, permitting pipeline input, marking mandatory parameters, and so on.

VerbSets

Ubiquitous Verbs	Data Verbs	Lifecycle Verbs	Diagnostics verb
Add	Checkpoint	Disable	Debug
Clear	Compare	Enable	Measure
Copy	Convert	Install	Ping
Get	Export	Restart	Resolve
Lock	Import	Resume	Test
Move	Initialize	Start	Trace
New	Limit	Stop	
Remove	Merge	Suspend	
Rename	Restore	Uninstall	
Set	Update		
Unlock			

13

Early thinking on PowerShell's approved verbs. Verbs are still grouped into these "sets" today, helping organize them by function.

Extended Reflection – Drill In

- Enables pipelines of structured data
- Allows access to properties or property paths (e.g. object navigation)
  - E.g. Exename.Version.FileVersion.Major
  - Each section could be:
    - Property/Field
    - Method (with parameters)
    - Xpath specification (for XML docs)
    - Brokered method
- Named sets of properties simplifies the user experience
  - E.g. ConfigurationSet, HealthSet, PerformanceSet, ResourceSet, SecuritySet
  - ConfigurationSet
    - NIC => Name, DeviceID, AutoSense, MACAddress, Speed
    - Service =>Name, DesktopInteract, PathName, StartMode.ServiceType,AcceptPause, AcceptStop
- Uniform way to perform formatting Name[:FormatString[:AsName]]
  - E.g. CreationTime:yy-mm-dd:Birthday
- Allows extension of types
  - E.g. Ipaddress.Netview.24HourHealth or Server.Unicenter.ServiceContract.SupportContact
  - Specify a key for a type to enable comparisons

15

A drill-down into the pipeline, and how it would pass structured objects from command to command. We again see a reference to the never-fully-realized PropertySets. Uniform formatting capabilities are mentioned, and the Extensible Type System is once again hinted at.

Hula Monkey

In the v1 and v2 days, Microsoft was using some admittedly antiquated source-control software. It was so antiquated that the developers could easily create conflicts if two people tried to check in code at the same time.

Their workaround was eminently pragmatic: a Hula Monkey.

The Hula Monkey, seen in a display case of Monad and PowerShell memorabilia on Microsoft's campus in Redmond, WA

Formed from coconuts into the shape of a monkey, and obviously wearing a hula skirt, Hula Monkey sported a McDonalds-style "Golden Arches" logo, with the "M" standing for "Monad" and the fast food chain's "I'm Lovin' It" slogan written underneath.

When a developer needed to check in code, they'd poke their heads out of their office and into the hallway and yell, "who has Hula Monkey?" By convention, only the developer physically in possession of Hula Monkey could check-in code, thus eliminating potential conflicts.

Personalities

The thing to *always* remember about the PowerShell team is that they're *people*. People come with personalities, and that can make teams crazy, better, fun, and terrifying—all at once.

Ken Hansen shared some of his memories of some of the team's major personalities:

> The PowerShell team had a group of very different personalities… all passionate about the product! I think it was that combination that really created the eventual product and success. I just think the people involved made all the difference in this project. So a quick summation of some examples…
>
> Jeffrey Snover—along with being the originating genius and chief cheerleader and scary developer… by example and precept he set up the team to be supportive of new ideas and to have challenging discussions. He fostered an environment where the idea was the important thing—not just the words or reputation or something. In a very practical way he let 1,000 flowers bloom and then we'd whack down those that weren't working. He was very open to being challenged (which we did a lot of) and was able to create something even better from any discussion.
>
> Bruce Payette—his encyclopedic knowledge of languages was key to developing PowerShell. In addition, he had this open way of exploring ideas. Many times I would come in with an idea and he would say, "yes, that's like <snowball or whatever> where they do <xyz>," and then he'd explain all the good things and the bad things

about that design. From there it was an open discussion on how to adopt the good parts, mitigate the bad parts and do it in a PowerShell-esque way.

Jim Truher—speaking of PowerShell-esque, in my mind one of Jim's great contributions to PowerShell was his ability to just say "no," and be absolutely hard-assed when it came to making it PowerShell-esque. Given the very broad range of scenarios we were trying to address with PowerShell, it was vital to maintain a common "flow." Personally I think it comes from his being an orchestra conductor.

Lee Holmes—probably the most even tempered person on the team (and on most teams I have seen). The word "colleague" keeps coming to mind. He provides this super-thoughtful space for ideas. He patiently explains both concepts and practices and thoughtfully explores new ideas easily.

June Blender—I don't remember the exact timeframe when June came to the project, but over time her impact was significant. We'd always believed in documentation, but she made it happen. Her insisting on getting every little detail right and understood could drive you nuts (completely nuts), as she'd come back again and again until it was right, but then *whammo*, great stuff just happened. The docs were rigorous and she wrote the code and loved the product and even became a really good speaker (even if she was always very nervous— which just made her prep all the more).

There are other personalities—Daryl, Hilal, etc—but I thought I'd at least start with these strong influences. It seems they were key to the product we created. We all know by experience that teams are really about people, and I think that new products tend to be imbued with the personalities of their creators.

www.ingramcontent.com/pod-product-compliance
Lightning Source LLC
Chambersburg PA
CBHW071208210326

41597CB00016B/1720